CLIFFSQUICKREVIEW®

Criminal Justice

By Dennis Hoffman

Wiley Publishing, Inc.

About the Author
Dennis E. Hoffman, Ph.D., teaches criminal justice at the University of Nebraska at Omaha.

Publisher's Acknowledgments
Editorial
Editors: Michelle Spence, Linda S. Stark
Acquisitions Editor: Kris Fulkerson
Composition
Indexer: York Production Services, Inc.
Proofreader: York Production Services, Inc.
Wiley Indianapolis Composition Services

CliffsQuickReview® *Criminal Justice*

Published by:
Wiley Publishing, Inc.
111 River Street
Hoboken, NJ 07030
www.wiley.com

CONTENTS

CONTENTS

CONTENTS

CONTENTS

CONTENTS

CONTENTS

CONTENTS

CONTENTS

CONTENTS

CONTENTS

CONTENTS

CONTENTS

CONTENTS

CONTENTS

CONTENTS

CONTENTS

PREFACE

Even the brightest college student can contract a bad case of information overload in dealing with the huge introductory-level texts in criminal justice. This book is intended to give you a remedy to relieve, counteract, and even prevent that problem by providing each of the following features:

- Because criminal justice research is ever-changing, even the best texts contain obsolete information within a few years. While there is no cure-all for the problem, in *CliffsQuickReview Criminal Justice,* you can find information on the cutting-edge research projects, the most recent Supreme Court rulings, and the state-of-the-art innovations in criminal justice.

- This book concentrates on the fundamentals of criminal justice, concisely and clearly, which allows you to find information quickly.

- Subjects such as capital punishment, gun control, and the drug war are hotly debated in criminal justice. *CliffsQuickReview Criminal Justice* discusses and examines the great debates in criminal justice by listing and explaining current arguments on both sides of the issues. Commentary on the great debates is provided at the end of each chapter to help you prepare for tests and think critically about matters of great public concern.

You'll find reference to the drug war intertwined with discussions of many subjects in this book because without question, the United States's main weapon in that war is the criminal justice system and because the handling of drug violations involves enormous expenditures of time and money (approximately $35 billion a year). While media portrayals often distort and sensationalize the realities of criminal justice, this book gives you a plain, unvarnished view of the justice system and of the politics of criminal justice.

The Structure of Criminal Justice

The phrase **criminal justice system** refers to a collection of federal, state, and local public agencies that deal with the crime problem. These agencies process suspects, defendants, and convicted offenders and are interdependent insofar as the decisions of one agency affect other agencies. The basic framework of the system is provided by the legislative, judicial, and executive branches of government.

The legislature
Legislatures, both state and federal, define crimes, fix sentences, and provide funding for criminal justice agencies.

The judiciary
Trial courts **adjudicate** (make judgments on and pronounce) the guilt of persons charged with crimes, and appellate courts interpret the law according to constitutional principles. Both state and federal appellate courts review legislative decisions and decide whether they fall within the boundaries of state law, federal law, and ultimately, the United States Constitution. **Judicial review** gives the courts the power to evaluate legislative acts in terms of whether they conform to the Constitution. If a law is in conflict with the Constitution, an appellate court may strike it down.

The executive branch
Executive power is given to the president, governors, and mayors. On criminal justice matters, they have the power to appoint judges and heads of agencies, such as police chiefs and directors of departments

of corrections. In addition, elected officials can lead efforts to improve criminal justice by putting forth legislative agendas and mobilizing public opinion.

The major components of the justice system

The justice system's major components—police, courts, and corrections—prevent or deter crime by apprehending, trying, and punishing offenders.

Police departments are public agencies whose purposes are to maintain order, enforce the criminal law, and provide services. Police officers operate in the community to prevent and control crime. They cooperate with prosecutors in criminal investigations, gathering evidence necessary to obtain convictions in the courts.

Courts are tribunals where persons accused of violating criminal law come to have their criminal responsibility determined by juries or judges. The purposes of the courts are to seek justice and to discover the truth. The primary actors in the courts are the prosecutors, defense attorneys, and judges.

Corrections include probation, parole, jail, prison, and a variety of new community-based sanctions, such as electronic monitoring and house arrest. The purposes of correctional agencies are to punish, to rehabilitate, and to ensure public safety.

The differences between federal and state justice systems

Federal and state justice systems carry out the same functions (enforcing laws, trying cases, and punishing offenders), but the laws and agencies of the two systems differ. State legislatures make most criminal laws, which are enforced by state and local police. City and county prosecutors try persons accused of breaking state laws in state courts. Judges sentence offenders convicted of violating state laws to serve time in either locally supervised jails or state-controlled correctional institutions. At the federal level, Congress enacts criminal laws,

and federal law enforcement agencies, such as the Federal Bureau of Investigation, enforce these laws. U.S. attorneys prosecute persons accused of committing federal crimes, and U.S. courts try the cases. To punish and rehabilitate those convicted of federal crimes, the Federal Bureau of Prisons provides programs and institutions.

The first line of defense against crime

The administration of justice in the United States is mainly a state and local affair. State and local governments employ two-thirds of all criminal justice workers and also pay a much larger share of the costs of criminal justice than the federal government. Then, too, state, county, and city criminal justice agencies provide most of the protection from thieves, rapists, and murderers.

Criminal justice as a nonsystem

Critics say criminal justice is really *not* a system. They point out that in some respects criminal justice agencies are independent bodies and that they take their authority and budgets from different sources. Police departments are funded mainly by towns and cities; prosecutors, public defenders, trial courts, and jails are mainly countywide; and prisons and appellate courts are mainly statewide. In addition to having separate sources of authority and funding, criminal justice agencies set their own policies. Finally, the agencies often fail to coordinate their activities and, thereby, ignore the impact that their decisions will have on other agencies.

The Process of Criminal Justice

Criminal justice is a process, involving a series of steps beginning with a criminal investigation and ending with the release of a convicted offender from correctional supervision. Rules and decision making are at the center of this process.

Rules

Sources of rules in criminal justice include the U.S. Constitution and Bill of Rights, state constitutions, the U.S. Code, state codes, court decisions, federal rules of criminal procedure, state rules of criminal procedure, and department and agency rules and regulations. The Federal Rules of Criminal Procedure, for example, govern the procedure in all criminal proceedings in courts of the United States.

Discretion

Decision making in criminal justice involves more than the learning of rules and the application of them to specific cases. Decisions are based on discretion, that is, the individual exercise of judgment to make choices about alternative courses of action. Discretion, or making decisions without formal rules, is common in criminal justice. Discretion comes into play whenever police make choices about whether to arrest, investigate, search, question, or use force. Similarly, prosecutors exercise individual judgment in deciding whether to charge a person with a crime and whether to plea-bargain. Judges also use discretion when setting bail, accepting or rejecting plea bargains, ruling on pretrial motions, and sentencing. Parole board members exercise discretion when deciding whether and when to release inmates from prison.

Steps in the criminal justice process

The major steps in processing a criminal case are as follows:

1. **Investigation** of a crime by the police. The purpose of a criminal investigation is to gather evidence to identify a suspect and support an arrest. An investigation may require a **search,** an exploratory inspection of a person or property. **Probable cause** is the standard of proof required for a search. Probable cause means there are facts or apparent facts indicating that evidence of criminality can be found in a specific place.

2. **Arrest** of a suspect by the police. An arrest involves taking a person into custody for the purpose of holding the suspect until court. **Probable cause** is the legal requirement for an arrest. It means that there is a reasonable link between a specific person and a particular crime.

3. **Prosecution** of a criminal defendant by a district attorney. When deciding whether to charge a person with a crime, prosecutors weigh many factors, including the seriousness of the offense and the strength of the evidence.

4. **Indictment** by a grand jury or the filing of an **information** by a prosecutor. Under the Federal Rules of Criminal Procedure, an indictment is required when prosecuting a capital offense. A prosecutor has the option of an indictment or an information in cases involving crimes punishable by imprisonment. In about half the states and the federal system, a grand jury decides whether to bring charges against a person in a closed hearing in which only the prosecutor presents evidence. The defendant has no right to be present at grand jury proceedings and no right to have a defense attorney represent him or her before the grand jury. The standard for indicting a person for a crime is **probable cause.** In the remaining states, a prosecutor files a charging document called an **information.** A preliminary (probable cause) hearing is held to determine if there is enough evidence to warrant a trial. The defendant and his or her attorney can be present at this hearing to dispute the charges.

5. **Arraignment** by a judge. Before the trial, the defendant appears in court and enters a plea. The most common pleas are guilty and not guilty.

6. **Pretrial detention** and/or **bail.** Detention refers to a period of temporary custody prior to trial. Bail is an amount of money paid by a defendant to ensure he or she will show up for a trial.

7. **Plea bargaining** between the defense attorney and the prosecutor. Usually, in plea bargaining, the defendant agrees to plead guilty in exchange for a charge reduction or sentence reduction.

8. **Trial/adjudication of guilt** by a judge or jury, with a prosecutor and a defense attorney participating. A trial is held before a judge or jury. The standard of evidence for a criminal conviction is **guilt beyond a reasonable doubt**—less than 100 percent certainty but more than high probability. If there is doubt based on reason, the accused is entitled to be acquitted.

9. **Sentencing** by a judge. If the accused is found guilty, a judge metes out a sentence. Possible sentences include a fine, probation, a period of incarceration in a correctional institution, such as a jail or prison, or some combination of supervision in the community and incarceration.

10. **Appeals** filed by attorneys in appellate courts and then ruled on by appellate judges. If an appellate court reverses a case, the case returns to trial court for retrial. With a reversal, the original trial becomes **moot** (that is, it is as though it never happened). Following a reversal, a prosecutor decides whether to refile or drop the charges. Even if a prosecutor drops the charges, the defendant can still be prosecuted later as long as the statute of limitations for the crime the defendant is accused of committing hasn't run out. Such a statute imposes time limits on the government to try a case.

11. **Punishment** and/or **rehabilitation** administered by local, state, or federal correctional authorities. Most inmates do *not* serve the complete term and are released before the expiration of their maximum sentences. Release may be obtained by serving the maximum sentence mandated by a court or through an early release mechanism, such as parole or pardon.

The criminal justice funnel and the Constitution

The criminal justice process is like a funnel, wide at the top and narrow at the bottom. Early in the criminal justice process, there are many cases, but the number of cases dwindles as decision makers remove cases from the process. Some cases are dismissed, while others are referred for treatment or counseling. Another way of expressing the funnel effect is to say that there are many more suspects and defendants than inmates. As criminal justice scholar Joel Samaha notes, the U.S. Constitution requires the government to support every deprivation of privacy, life, liberty, or property with facts. The greater the deprivation, the more facts that government agents are required to produce. A stop on the street requires fewer facts than an arrest; an arrest requires fewer facts than an indictment; an indictment requires fewer facts than a criminal conviction.

The Politics of Criminal Justice

Politics is the process by which resources are distributed or allocated. As a famous political scientist once remarked, "Politics is who gets what, when, and how." Political considerations are a necessary but sometimes problematic part of criminal justice.

Politics of selecting decision makers

Criminal justice decision makers are selected through election or appointment. In some states, voters elect judges, while in other states, governors appoint them. In either case, the selection process is political. Lawyers who have performed political deeds for their party often become candidates for judgeships. As for federal judges, the president appoints them and the Senate confirms them. The political process profoundly influences the U.S. Supreme Court. Retirements from the Court and new appointments produce shifts in the Court's positions on criminal justice issues.

Politics of lawmaking

Perhaps the most important way that the democratic political system shapes criminal justice is through the lawmaking process: Politics influences the laws that legislatures enact. During the 1980s and 1990s, state legislators and the U.S. congressional representatives rushed to frame politically conservative get-tough sentencing laws. These laws mandate longer sentences and fewer opportunities for parole. One lawyer who was instrumental in rewriting federal drug laws in 1986 and 1988 says the severe sentencing laws came about through whim and attempts by politicians to one-up each other as drugs seized media headlines just before elections. "There was a level of hysteria that led to a total breakdown of the legislative process," says the lawyer, Eric Sterling, who as lead attorney on the U.S. House Committee on the Judiciary wrote the laws that established long mandatory sentences for several types of drug convictions.

What has resulted from two decades of get-tough sentencing policy? The prison population has exploded. Costs of corrections have skyrocketed. The distribution of revenue within state governments has shifted in favor of allocating more money for prisons and less for education and other essential human services.

Politics and policing

Even though politics doesn't have a direct impact on the routine, daily decisions of police officers on patrol, the political culture of a community determines the style of law enforcement and the nature of departmental policy. Form of government (commissioner, mayor/council, city manager) makes a difference in the extent to which politics shape policing. Politics permeates police departments in cities that employ a mayor/council type of government. By contrast, a professional city manager makes political intervention into policing less likely.

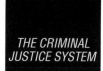

Politics of prosecution
Political considerations influence prosecutors in a direct way.
Prosecutors are elected in most states and are heavily involved in
local politics. At the federal level, U.S. attorneys are political
appointees and tend to mesh their career ambitions to the needs of
their political party. Both state and federal prosecutors often use their
office as a springboard for higher political office. Occasionally, an
unscrupulous prosecutor will abuse power in the worst way: Acting
on the basis of political motives, the prosecutor will engage in **political prosecutions** by pressing criminal charges against political enemies. A case can be made, for example, that independent counsel
Kenneth Starr's conservative politics motivated his investigations of
President Clinton's extramarital affairs during the late 1990s.

Politics of judicial decision-making
Judges experience tremendous political pressure. Questionable political influences come into play when judges are faced with the decision of whether or not to impose the death penalty. It isn't a
coincidence that elected judges impose the death penalty at higher
rates than appointed judges. This difference stems from elected
judges' fear of appearing soft on crime. Refusing to impose the death
penalty makes a judge vulnerable to attacks from political opponents
who may use the judge's decision against him or her at the next judicial retention election.

Politics of corrections
Corrections officials also take political considerations into account.
Politics can drive a parole board's release decisions. Parole board
members are susceptible to influence from the governors who appoint
them. Members almost inevitably make release decisions cautiously.
If parolees commit crimes, the media, the governor's political rivals,
or both may blame the governor.

Politicization of criminal justice

Serious problems for citizens and the criminal justice system can result from the politicization of criminal justice, a process through which political leaders seize opportunities to use criminal justice issues to enhance their own popularity, electability, or power. Politicization can be observed most readily in political campaigns in which law-and-order rhetoric is prevalent. When criminal justice issues become too politicized, politicians are tempted to engage in **demagoguery,** appealing to people's emotions, passions, and prejudices rather than to people's minds. Political demagoguery is the enemy of clear thinking about solutions to the crime problem.

Politics of stymie

Unnecessary political wrangling over criminal justice issues—which can happen when winning political skirmishes becomes more important to public officials than controlling crime and achieving justice—can cripple the justice process. One undesirable result is that the justice process grinds to a halt. The U.S. Sentencing Commission had no members for the last three months of 1998 because Republicans and Democrats couldn't agree on selections to the seven slots on the commission. This commission, created by Congress in 1984, has as its main purpose the establishment of guidelines for meting out punishment for those convicted of federal crimes. It was started to reduce disparity in federal sentencing and to help develop effective and efficient crime policy.

Great Debates in Criminal Justice: Should the Crime
Control Model or the Due Process Model Prevail?

Herbert Packer, a Stanford University law professor, constructed two models, the **crime control model** and the **due process model,** to represent the two competing systems of values operating within

THE CRIMINAL
JUSTICE SYSTEM

criminal justice. The tension between the two accounts for the conflict and disharmony that now is observable in the criminal justice system.

The crime control model should prevail

The following assertions are the key concerns of the crime control model:

1. The repression of crime should be the most important function of criminal justice because order is a necessary condition for a free society.

2. Criminal justice should concentrate on vindicating victims' rights rather than on protecting defendants' rights.

3. Police powers should be expanded to make it easier to investigate, arrest, search, seize, and convict.

4. Legal technicalities that handcuff the police should be eliminated.

5. The criminal justice process should operate like an assembly-line conveyor belt, moving cases swiftly along toward their disposition.

6. If the police make an arrest and a prosecutor files criminal charges, the accused should be presumed guilty because the fact-finding of police and prosecutors is highly reliable.

7. The main objective of the criminal justice process should be to discover the truth or to establish the factual guilt of the accused.

The due process model should prevail

Packer's due process model is a counterproposal to the crime control model. It consists of these arguments:

CRIMINAL JUSTICE

11

1. The most important function of criminal justice should be to provide due process, or fundamental fairness under the law.

2. Criminal justice should concentrate on defendants' rights, not victims' rights, because the Bill of Rights expressly provides for the protection of defendants' rights.

3. Police powers should be limited to prevent official oppression of the individual.

4. Constitutional rights aren't mere technicalities; criminal justice authorities should be held accountable to rules, procedures, and guidelines to ensure fairness and consistency in the justice process.

5. The criminal justice process should look like an obstacle course, consisting of a series of impediments that take the form of procedural safeguards that serve as much to protect the factually innocent as to convict the factually guilty.

6. The government shouldn't hold a person guilty solely on the basis of the facts; a person should be found guilty only if the government follows legal procedures in its fact-finding.

Evaluating the crime control and due process models
To declare that one of these models is superior to the other requires one to make a value judgment. The crime control model reflects conservative values, while the due process model reflects liberal values. Political climate determines which model shapes criminal justice policy at a specific time. During the politically liberal 1960s, the principles and policies of due process predominated in criminal justice. From the mid 1970s to the early twenty-first century, conservatism has held sway as the dominant political philosophy, and conservatives have formulated criminal justice policies in the image of the crime control model.

CHAPTER 2
CRIMINAL JUSTICE IN THE U.S.

In a democracy, we strive to strike a balance between freedom and order. Imposing crime control measures may make us feel safer but also may endanger our civil liberties. Seeking to keep these competing democratic values in a state of equilibrium is a constant struggle. This ongoing conflict between crime control and due process values takes place within the context of a justice system that is unique in the world.

Citizen Participation

Citizens, often a forgotten component of criminal justice, play a variety of important roles in American justice, and their involvement is crucial to the functioning of the justice system in a democratic society.

Lobbying elected officials

Citizens affect criminal justice policy through **interest groups.** Representatives of interest groups lobby lawmakers to pass legislation favoring the interests of the groups they represent. Michael Hallett and Dennis Palumbo, criminal justice scholars, discovered that many big and powerful interest groups get involved in legislative lobbying at the federal level. The American Bar Association, the American Civil Liberties Union, and business groups such as the U.S. Chamber of Commerce have the most influence at this level. Some single-issue groups, such as the National Rifle Association (NRA), also exercise political clout on certain issues. At the state level, Hallett and Palumbo point out, criminal justice policy is made by small numbers of influential state legislators, administrators of criminal justice agencies, and representatives of criminal justice professionals. Interest groups having the most influence are those representing police and prosecutors.

Influencing judicial policymaking

Poor people and racial minority citizens exert more influence over the appellate courts, such as the U.S. Supreme Court, than they do over legislation. Representatives of disadvantaged groups influence court decisions by filing *amicus curiae* (friend of the court) briefs in cases. These briefs present legal arguments or facts on behalf of others.

Raising public consciousness

Interest groups raise the consciousness of the public and elected officials about criminal justice issues. One example is the National Organization for Women (NOW). It has made people aware of the problems of battered women and has succeeded in getting policy changes that made domestic violence a crime rather than a family matter.

Performing jury duty

American criminal justice exhibits a strong commitment to a jury of lay persons. Juries provide important protections against the abuse of power by legislatures, judges, and other powerful entities; bring broadly based community values to deciding criminal cases; inject common sense into criminal justice decision making; and afford citizens opportunities to learn about the law and the justice process.

Reporting crimes and testifying in criminal cases

Citizen cooperation is absolutely necessary for the apprehension and prosecution of criminals. Almost all criminal proceedings have a lay witness who is a citizen bystander or victim possessing personal knowledge that is relevant to a criminal case.

Establishing and conducting mediation

Many communities in the United States have created reparative boards. **Reparative boards** remove cases from the criminal courts and resolve cases through mediation in a nonadversarial manner. They are designed to save money, allow victims to participate in the justice process, and reintegrate offenders into communities.

Monitoring the criminal justice system

Civilian review boards consist of persons who aren't police officers and who assess how police departments handle citizen complaints. The boards may recommend remedial action, but they don't have the power to investigate or discipline police officers. Three-fourths of America's largest cities have civilian review. **Citizens' crime commissions** are independent, privately funded agencies that serve as public watchdogs—they observe judges in courtrooms, investigate corruption throughout the justice system, and conduct research on the administration of justice. These commissions operate in more than 20 metropolitan areas in the United States.

Providing statements about harm caused by criminals

Victims of crime may influence judges' sentencing decisions. Aggravating circumstances affect sentencing, and often **victim impact statements** convince a judge to give the maximum sentence. These statements are a method of informing a judge about the harm caused by the crime in question. Critics argue that allowing the victim or members of the victim's family to testify at sentencing as to the harm an offender has caused is tantamount to allowing vengeance to drive the sentencing process.

Rights Consciousness and Civil Liberties

Americans are very conscious of their rights. **Individual rights** are rights that the government cannot abridge. Often, citizens don't know the content of specific rights, but they assert their entitlement to those rights anyway.

General versus specific rights

Belief in a **specific right** spurred a convicted felon, Clarence Gideon, to contest his conviction. The U.S. Supreme Court used this appeal as a means in *Gideon v. Wainwright* (1963) to establish an indigent defendant's right to an attorney at felony trials.

A **general right** can have applications beyond the case in which it is first established. The right to privacy, for example, has played a part in thousands of cases dealing with police procedures for conducting searches and seizures. Another general right is the right to be treated fairly. Americans are very conscious of their due process rights because so many rights are related to the procedures by which the government can take away life, liberty, and property.

The Bill of Rights

The main source of citizens' rights in America is the Bill of Rights, the first ten amendments to the Constitution. The Bill of Rights, which took effect in 1791, details the rights of the American people and forbids the government to violate those rights. Four of the amendments pertain directly to criminal justice. These amendments depict procedural rights that apply to citizens accused of crime, defendants in criminal cases, and inmates in jails and prisons.

- The **Fourth Amendment** prohibits the government from conducting "unreasonable searches and seizures."

- The **Fifth Amendment** provides the privilege against self-incrimination, forbids the government to try a person twice for the same offense **(double jeopardy),** and promises "due process of law."

- The **Sixth Amendment** sets out the requirements for criminal trials, including the defendant's right to counsel.

- The **Eighth Amendment** forbids the government to subject inmates to "cruel and unusual punishments."

Originally, the Bill of Rights imposed restrictions upon only the federal government. It provided no protection to citizens against state or local action.

The Fourteenth Amendment and due process

After the Civil War, the Fourteenth Amendment, ratified in 1868, was added to the Constitution. It bars states from violating people's right to due process of law. It states that "no State shall . . . deprive any person of life, liberty, or property, without due process of law; nor deny to any person within its jurisdiction the equal protection of the laws." These rights of due process and equal protection were intended to protect individuals from abusive actions by state and local criminal justice officials. The terms "due process" and "equal protection" were left to the Supreme Court to define.

Earl Warren and the due process revolution

During Earl Warren's tenure as chief justice of the Supreme Court (1953–1969), the Court raised Americans' consciousness of their constitutional rights and adopted a liberal rights agenda, including freedom of speech, equality of minorities, and due process rights for defendants. Warren and his liberal brethren on the Court used the due process clause of the Fourteenth Amendment to nationalize the Bill of Rights. The **due process clause** stipulates that the government cannot take any citizen's life, liberty, or property without due process. The Warren Court broke with Court precedent that the Bill of Rights provided no protection against state or local action, but only against federal authority. It held that the due process clause did, indeed, apply to state and local governments. In a series of landmark decisions, the Court selectively incorporated certain provisions of the Bill of Rights and made them binding upon the states. The Court extended the Fourth, Fifth, Sixth, and Eighth Amendments to defendants in state criminal proceedings. This extension radically changed criminal justice as practiced in state and local governments by increasing individual rights in state and local criminal cases. Scholars refer to the Warren Court's expansion of the rights of criminal defendants and the application of the rights to state proceedings as the "due process revolution."

Due process rights

The question at the heart of Earl Warren's approach to law during his 16 years as Chief Justice was "Is it fair?" This question captures the essence of due process. A basic principle of American criminal justice is that the government should treat people fairly. The Fifth and Fourteenth Amendments prohibit the government from depriving a person of life, liberty, or property "without due process of law." Due process of law includes court procedures that protect persons accused of wrongdoing. For example:

- The government cannot force a person to testify against himself or herself.

- Citizens must be informed of the charges against them.

- Citizens may demand a jury trial, which must be held soon after charges are filed.

- If citizens cannot afford a lawyer, the government must provide one.

- Persons on trial may cross-examine their accusers and may force witnesses to testify.

Individual versus group rights

Whereas due process rights are **individual rights,** or **civil liberties** (in other words, rights as guarantees to a person against government interference), other rights are classified as **group rights.** Debate over the issue of racial equality in the mid-20th century led Americans to become more conscious not only of individual rights but also of group rights. After the Warren Court's landmark ruling in **Brown v. Board of Education** (1954) requiring equal treatment regardless of race in schools, the need to consider remedies for segregation and racial discrimination focused attention on an individual's position as a member of a group—and thus on group rights. According to legal scholar Stephen Wasby, this shift was part of a change in concern from civil liberties to **civil rights** (in other words, rights as guarantees of equal treatment for all people). Civil rights include the right of all people to receive equal protection of the law. As Wasby points out, the extension of civil rights consciousness from African-Americans to other groups also increased Americans' awareness of group rights. Group rights matter in criminal justice because criminal laws and criminal justice practices can be discriminatory in their effects on whole categories of people.

Racial Disparities in American Criminal Justice

The United States is a multiracial, multiethnic society. The major racial/ethnic categories in American society are white, African-American, Hispanic, Asian, and Native American. **Racism,** an insidious social problem in the United States since the founding of the country, is the belief that members of one or more races are inferior to members of other races. Racism in the United States has been directed primarily by the white majority against racial and ethnic minorities. Historically, the white majority has singled out racial/ethnic minority groups for differential and unequal treatment in the areas of housing, employment, education, and criminal justice.

The meaning of racial disparity
The term **racial disparity** refers to a difference that may or may *not* be related to discrimination. Criminal justice experts distinguish between legal and extralegal factors to explain racial disparities in

criminal justice. **Legal factors** include seriousness of the offense and prior criminal record. These are legitimate reasons for disparities because they pertain to an individual's criminal behavior. **Extralegal factors** include race, class, and gender. These are *not* legitimate factors upon which to base decisions because they relate to group membership rather than criminal behavior.

Types of racial disparities

One type of racial disparity occurs when there is a significant difference between the percentage of a racial group represented in the general population and the percentage of the same group represented at any point in the justice process. For example, African-Americans make up 12 percent of the U.S. population but account for about 40 percent of all arrests, 50 percent of the prison population, and 50 percent of the inmates on death row. Another type of racial disparity appears whenever there is a significantly larger percentage of members of a racial/minority group involved in a part of the criminal justice system than whites. For instance, more than 9 percent of all African-American adult males are in jail or prison or on probation or parole, compared with not quite 2 percent of all white adult males. To cite another example, blacks are four times as likely as whites to be arrested on drug charges—even though the two groups use drugs at almost the same rate.

The reasons racial disparities exist

Racial disparities in criminal justice are explained in three ways: differential involvement, individual racism, and institutional racism. First, African-Americans and Hispanics are **differentially involved** in criminality—they commit more crimes. Their criminality is tied to the fact that these groups suffer from poverty and unemployment. Second, some of the disparities are due to the bigotry of individual police officers, prosecutors, defense attorneys, judges, probation officers, parole officers, and parole board members. This **individual**

racism consists of prejudicial beliefs and discriminatory behavior of individual criminal justice authorities against blacks and other minority group members. Third, part of the disparities can be attributed to **institutional racism.** This type of racism occurs whenever there are statutes, classifications, and practices that have a "disparate (unequal) impact" on racial minorities.

Great Debates in Criminal Justice:
Is the Criminal Justice System Racist?

American society is becoming more racially and economically polarized. Many poor and minority citizens subscribe to the **discrimination thesis** (DT) that the criminal justice system is racist. A recent Gallup poll showed that nearly two-thirds of the African-Americans surveyed believe that the criminal justice system is rigged against them. Many civil rights advocacy groups agree, but many conservatives deny that the system is racist.

The criminal justice system is not racist

Criminologist William Wilbanks, who wrote *The Myth of a Racist Criminal Justice System* (1987), is the leading apologist for racial disparities in the American justice system. Wilbanks and others who maintain the system is color blind advance the following arguments:

1. Most decisions in criminal justice are *not* based on discrimination. Research demonstrates that decisions throughout the justice systems are based mainly on the seriousness of the crime, the amount of legal evidence proving guilt that is available, and the prior criminal record of the suspect, defendant, or inmate.

2. There is no **systematic racism** in criminal justice. Wilbanks coined the phrase "systematic racism" and uses it as an ideal standard against which to measure American criminal justice. In disproving the discrimination thesis, he wraps the complex question of racial discrimination into two bundles labeled "The Criminal Justice System Is Racist" and "The Criminal Justice System Is Not Racist." He says either there is discrimination in *all* parts of the criminal justice system (for example, in the police, courts, and corrections) and in *all* stages of the criminal justice process or there is *no* racial discrimination in the system. After reviewing the scholarly literature, Wilbanks concludes that the criminal justice system is not racist because the evidence fails to prove that racism is present in all parts of the system during all steps of the criminal justice process.

The criminal justice system is racist

In *The Color of Justice* (1996), Samuel Walker, Cassia Spohn, and Miriam DeLone avoid what critics see as the mistake of treating the complex problem of racial discrimination as if it could be divided into two simple extremes. They say

1. "The criminal justice system is neither completely free of racial bias nor systematically biased." Drawing from hundreds of studies of race and criminal justice, Walker and his colleagues take the middle ground. They argue that racial/ethnic groups are treated more harshly than whites at some stages in the system but no differently from whites at other stages.

2. Solid evidence of discrimination exists in many stages of the criminal justice process, including the police use of deadly force and the application of the death penalty.

3. Drug policies constitute the single most significant factor contributing to racial disparities in criminal justice. Federal cocaine laws are a prime example of institutional racism. Under the current law, crimes involving crack-cocaine are punished much more severely than those involving powder-cocaine. The federal guidelines consider a given amount of crack the same as a hundred times the amount of powder-cocaine. This hundred-to-one ratio produces sentences for crack defendants that are far more severe than sentences for defendants whose crimes involve powder-cocaine. The problem is that black cocaine users prefer crack, while white users like powder. African-American defendants have argued in federal courts that the guidelines discriminate on the basis of race and violate the equal protection clause of the Fourteenth Amendment. Among the statistics offered in support of this claim are those showing that of all the persons charged with possession of crack-cocaine, most are black; in contrast, of those charged with possession of powder-cocaine, most are white.

Understanding racism in criminal justice

A consensus about racism exists among criminal justice administrators, policymakers, and academics: there should be zero tolerance for it in the administration of justice. The conclusion that racial discrimination is absolute, complete, or omnipresent in the justice system certainly does *not* follow from the research on the subject. But a majority of scholars would certainly agree that there is a substantial body of evidence proving that racial bias inheres in certain practices and policies of both the criminal justice and juvenile justice systems.

CHAPTER 3
CRIME

The crime was horrific enough: cunningly cruel, brutal, and senseless. But it was the way the victim was chosen—singled out apparently because he was a homosexual—that aroused the American people. The murder in 1998 of Matthew Shepard shocked the nation. The slashing and bludgeoning of Shepard in rural Wyoming set off new calls for a hate-crime law in Wyoming and for passage of federal hate-crime legislation.

There are strong arguments both for and against **hate-crime laws.** Advocates argue that these laws make the symbolic statement that there will be zero tolerance for harmful acts motivated by sexism, racism, or homophobia. By contrast, critics of hate-crime laws say they violate the First Amendment right to freedom of speech.

Criminal law has historically avoided punishing people for their thoughts, and that is what hate-crime laws seem to do. Opponents claim that punishing people for being bigots is really no different from punishing them for their political beliefs. While conceding that crimes are reprehensible when they are motivated by hate, critics assert that this distinction should not be written into criminal law.

Being an informed citizen who is able to participate intelligently in debates such as this one requires a clear understanding of the nature of crime in the United States.

Definitions of Crime

Criminologist Paul Tappan defines **crime** as "an intentional act or omission in violation of criminal law . . ., committed without defense or justification, and sanctioned by the state as a felony or misdemeanor."

Misdemeanors and felonies

Possible punishments determine the differences between misdemeanors and felonies. **Misdemeanors** are nonserious, minor crimes that the government punishes by confinement in a local jail for a year or less. Examples include petty theft, simple assault, disorderly conduct, and disturbing the peace. **Felonies** are serious crimes that the government punishes by death or incarceration in a prison for at least a year. This group includes such crimes as murder, rape, robbery, and burglary.

Crimes versus torts

A **crime,** or public wrong, is to be distinguished from a **tort,** or private wrong. Actually, the same act may be both a crime and a tort. For example, O. J. Simpson's alleged killings of Nicole Simpson and Ron Goldman included the torts of assault, battery, and wrongful death. Simpson's alleged acts gave rise to both a criminal prosecution (seeking punishment) and a civil suit for damages.

State and federal crimes

A notable difference between state and federal crimes is that federal crimes usually include a jurisdictional element. **Jurisdiction** refers to the geographic or substantive range of a court's authority. The U.S. Code, for example, doesn't punish theft itself. It punishes theft from an interstate shipment or theft of government property. Federal statutes exhibit a concern for jurisdiction because the Constitution limits Congress to enacting laws about subjects falling within its specific powers. The states maintain lawmaking authority not delegated to the federal government.

When both the federal government and a state can prosecute a person for the same incident, there is **overlapping jurisdiction.** The Constitution permits double prosecution in such cases. Take, for example, the Rodney King beating case. The state of California prosecuted four Los Angeles police officers for assault. After an all-white jury acquitted them, the federal government held a separate trial based on the same incident. In 1993, after an FBI investigation and federal prosecution, a multiracial jury convicted two of the officers of violating King's civil rights.

Types of Crime

The United States has more than a single crime problem. One problem is high, though currently declining, rates of street crime (including homicide, assault, rape, robbery, and burglary). Much of this type of crime is committed by an alienated and self-destructive underclass. Another is the drug-crime problem, which is linked to the first problem. Some drug-intoxicated individuals commit crimes because they have lost their inhibitions while under the influence.

There are also crimes that stem from the drug business (for example, money laundering) and crimes that arise from economic necessity, because users need money to buy more drugs. Then, too, there is the organized-crime problem, which is intertwined with the drug-crime problem insofar as drug trafficking is the major source of income for organized-crime groups. In addition, there is a white-collar-crime problem. It, too, is linked to other types of crime. For example, federal investigators uncovered a scheme in 1998 by two New York crime families and a half dozen Wall Street stockbrokers to commit stock fraud.

- **Drug crimes.** The drug-crime category encompasses a range of offenses connected with the use, transportation, purchase, and sale of illegal drugs.

- **Street crime.** The most common forms of predatory crime— rape, robbery, assault, burglary, larceny, and auto theft—occur most frequently on urban streets. Racial minority citizens account for a disproportionately high number of the arrests for street crimes.

- **Organized crime.** The term "organized crime" refers to the unlawful activities of members of criminal organizations that supply illegal goods and services.

- **Political crime.** The political-crime category contains both crimes by the government and crimes against the government. Political goals motivate political criminals.

- **Victimless crime.** Consensual acts (in which people are willing participants) and violations in which only the perpetrator is hurt, such as the personal use of illegal drugs, are called victimless crimes.

- **White-collar crime.** White-collar crimes are offenses that persons commit while acting in their legitimate jobs and professions. White-collar criminals behave in unethical ways for self-gain (for example, embezzlement) or for the benefit of a business (for example, corporate price-fixing). Victims of white-collar crime include the economy, employers, consumers, and the environment.

Part I Offenses

The Federal Bureau of Investigation (FBI) designates certain crimes as **Part I** or **index offenses** because it considers them to be the major crimes plaguing society in the United States.

- **Murder** is the unlawful killing of one human being by another. In 1996, 19,645 murders came to the attention of police departments in the United States. First-degree murder is premeditated, deliberate criminal homicide. Second-degree murder is an intentional killing that is generally unplanned and may happen "in the heat of passion." Firearms are the weapon of choice in most murders.

- **Forcible rape** is "the carnal knowledge of a female forcibly and against her will." Statutory rape differs from forcible rape in that it involves sex with a female who is under majority age. Forcible rape is the least reported of all violent crimes.

- **Robbery** is the unlawful taking or attempted taking of property that is in the possession of another, by force or the threat of force. Guns are fired in 20 percent of robberies.

- **Aggravated assault** involves the unlawful, intentional inflicting, or attempted or threatened inflicting, of injury upon another person. In an aggravated assault, the perpetrator either uses a weapon or hurts the victim so badly that the victim requires medical assistance.

- **Burglary** is unlawful entry of a structure, vehicle, or vessel without force, with intent to commit a felony.

- **Larceny-theft** is the unlawful taking or attempted taking of property from the possession of another, by stealth, without force, with intent to permanently deprive the owner of the property. It includes such crimes as shoplifting, pocket picking, purse snatching, and bike stealing. Larceny-theft makes up over 50 percent of the crime committed annually in the United States, making it the largest crime category.

- **Motor vehicle theft** is the unlawful taking or attempted taking of a vehicle owned by another with the intent to deprive the owner of it.

- **Arson** is the burning or attempted burning of property with or without the intent to defraud.

Sources of Information on Crime

Two sources of information, compiled by the federal government, provide data on crime in the United States. The FBI produces its annual **Uniform Crime Reports (UCR),** giving estimates of arrests and crimes reported to the police. The U.S. Justice Department also conducts an annual **National Crime Victimization Survey (NCVS),** which is the product of an annual random sampling of households. The Victimization Survey picks up crimes not reported to the police.

The UCR

The UCR reports Part I crimes in terms of both crimes known to the police and arrests. Part I crimes are reported in terms of arrests. Part II includes, but is not limited to, some victimless crimes. Since citizens often don't report victimless crimes and police find them difficult to detect, it makes sense to use arrest statistics for information on this type of crime. During 1996, law enforcement agencies made about 15 million arrests for Part II crimes. The highest arrest counts were for drug abuse violations, larceny-thefts, and driving under the influence, each at 1.5 million.

One of the UCR's key features is the **Crime Index,** which is the sum of Part I crimes for a given year. In 1996, the Crime Index was 13.5 million offenses. Nonviolent property crimes made up almost 90 percent of the total number of index offenses.

The **crime rate,** or the number of Part I offenses that occurred in a given area for every 100,000 people living in the area, is calculated as follows: total Crime Index divided by population multiplied by 100,000 equals crime rate. The UCR also figures crime rates for specific crimes. For example, the national murder rate in 1997 was 770 murders per 100,000 people.

What does it mean when the official Part I crime rate increases? One or more of three things can be happening:

- More people are committing crimes.

- Offenders have higher individual crime rates.

- A higher proportion of crimes committed are being reported or recorded.

An advantage of the UCR is that it includes homicides in its calculation of the violent crime rate (which the NCVS by its nature cannot). The main disadvantage of the UCR is that much crime is never reported to the police and never shows up in the UCR. Thus, UCR estimates of the volume and rates of crime are always lower than the actual frequencies of such occurrences because crime is subject to both nonreporting by citizens and nonrecording by the police. Trends in official statistics may be the result of changes in public reporting and police recording practices, not of actual changes in the amount of crime.

The NCVS
The NCVS is an ongoing survey of households that consists of interviews with 100,000 persons in 50,000 households twice each year. It asks residents of the United States about their victimizations from crime and reports on rape, sexual assault, robbery, both simple and aggravated assault, theft, household burglary, and motor vehicle theft. It omits murder and drug crimes. The latter is an important omission because a shift in criminal activity from an included crime (for example, burglary or robbery) to drug dealing would appear as a decrease in the overall crime rate when no actual decrease had occurred. NCVS data reveal the following facts about crime and victimization.

- The actual amount of crime is several times greater than the UCR shows.

- Crime touches about 23 million households in the United States each year.

- The total personal cost of crime to victims is about $13 billion each year.

- The chance of being the victim of a violent crime is much higher for young African-American males than for any other group of the population.

- Violent criminal victimizations are extremely rare events.

- Most crimes against individuals are absorbed by the victims without reporting them to the police.

Drawbacks to this report are that some people may incorrectly remember events as crimes that were not crimes and the high cost of door-to-door interviewing.

Crime Decreases

One of the bigger myths about crime is that it is always increasing. The 1998 UCR shows that serious crime fell across the nation in 1997, the sixth consecutive annual decrease. Violent crimes declined by 5 percent, led by 9 percent decreases in murders and robberies. Property crimes declined by 4 percent, led by an 8 percent drop in arson. Similarly, the NCVS shows that the number of violent crimes fell more than 9 percent in 1995. Violent victimizations dropped from 10.9 million in 1994 to 9.9 million in 1995. Property crimes continued a 20-year pattern of decreasing rates. Why is crime decreasing?

A strong economy

The booming economy of the 1990s has helped to reduce crime rates. It has provided legitimate jobs to some urban young people who had worked in the drug trade.

Changing demographics

The age distribution in the United States has been changing. In 1980, more than 20 million people were between 15 and 19 years old. By 1990, that population group had dropped to 17.5 million. Similar drops have occurred in the 20–24 age group, a group with a high crime potential. Overall, the nation is aging, and older men don't commit as much crime as younger men.

Police manipulation of crime data

Senior police officials around the nation voiced concern in 1998 that the sharp drop in crime in the 1990s had produced pressure on police departments to show ever-decreasing crime statistics. In 1998, charges were leveled against police officials in New York, Philadelphia, Atlanta, and Boca Raton for falsely reporting crime statistics.

A common thread running through many of the incidents of police officials' alteration of crime statistics is that police commanders responded to pressure from politicians, the media, and the public to lower crime rates by downgrading felonies by intentionally mislabeling felonies, such as aggravated assault and burglary, as misdemeanors. Such a practice deflates rates of serious crimes and inflates rates of nonserious crimes. Experts say they believe these incidents do *not* mean that the nationwide drop in crime is illusory. They point to the fact that victimization data, which are not subject to police manipulation, indicate the same downward trend as the FBI's UCR.

The decline in the crack market
Crack has played a key role in pushing rates of violent crime up and down. When crack arrived in New York City in 1985, it created a big market for users and dealers. It was sold in small amounts that gave an intense high that required users to constantly find more. Thousands of unskilled, unemployed men from New York's poor inner-city neighborhoods entered the crack business as sellers, and to protect themselves from business competitors, they acquired handguns. Due to the combination of the crack epidemic and the increased firepower of more handguns on the streets, instances of violent crime surged starting in 1985. Crime rates began to fall in 1991. The turning point came when youths began to turn against smoking or selling crack and police stepped up efforts to seize handguns from criminals and juveniles.

A cautionary caveat
Deadly violence by young people remains a pressing problem. A Department of Justice study shows that while the nation's overall

homicide rate fell in 1997 to its lowest level in three decades, the number of firearm homicides by young people is still very high. The report offers no explanation for this discrepancy, but criminologists point to the spread of illegal handguns among young people that began with the start of the crack epidemic around 1985 as a major reason for the continuing high level of violence. The number of firearm homicides committed by those in the U.S. who are 25 and older declined between 1980 and 1997, by about 50 percent. Those crimes committed by adults ages 18–24 actually increased during the period by about the same percentage. The 6,076 killings by this age group in 1997, though fewer than the all-time record of 8,171 gun homicides in 1993, is almost double the number reported in 1976, the year the FBI began compiling such statistics.

Drugs and Crime

The connection between drugs and crime is reflected in at least three types of crimes:

- Drug-defined crimes, such as the possession, use, or sale of controlled substances, which violates drug laws.

- Crimes committed by drug users to get money to buy more drugs or crimes committed by persons under the influence of drugs.

- Organized criminal activities, such as money laundering and political corruption, in support of the drug trade.

Crime is associated with drug use, but drugs usually don't cause crime. First, only a small percentage of burglaries and robberies are drug related. Second, studies of high-rate offenders show that many of them began their criminal careers before using drugs. Most experts agree that even if we could succeed in eliminating drug abuse, there would be only a small reduction in robberies, burglaries, and similar crimes.

The amount of illegal drug use

The 1995 National Household Survey (which collects self-reported information from 4,000 to 9,000 individuals each year) indicates that drug use has declined but that illegal drug use among teenagers (ages 12–17) increased from 1990 to 1995. A second survey, the 1995 Drug Use Forecasting (DUF) program (which collects urine specimens and self-reported data on drug use from arrested persons) reports that a majority of male arrestees in U.S. cities tested positive for drugs.

Drug laws

The first major drug law, the **Harrison Act** (1914), required persons dealing in opium, morphine, heroin, cocaine, and derivatives of these drugs to register with the federal government. The **Comprehensive Drug Abuse Prevention and Control Act** (1970) forms the basis of federal enforcement efforts today. This law sets up five schedules which classify narcotic drugs according to the abuse potential. In 1988, the U.S. Republican leadership stepped up the war on drugs. It passed the **Anti-Drug Abuse Act,** which substantially increased the penalties for recreational drug users. Other important federal drug laws include the **Crime Control Act** (1990) and the **Violent Crime Control and Law Enforcement Act** (1994). The former doubled the appropriations to state and local communities for drug enforcement and created drug-free school zones by increasing penalties for drug crimes occurring close to schools. The latter provided $245 million for rural anti-crime and drug efforts.

Alcohol abuse and crime

Even though the abuse of alcohol is rarely discussed in the same terms as the use of controlled substances, alcohol abuse has serious consequences for abusers as well as the criminal justice system. First, alcohol is often a factor in the commission of crimes, drunk driving being a prime example. Sometimes the use of alcohol lowers inhibitions and leads to other, serious crimes, such as criminal assaults. Second, the processing of alcohol-related crimes consumes large amounts of criminal justice resources. For example, between 1970 and 1992 arrests for drunk driving soared 200 percent across the United States. Today, police make about one million drunk driving arrests annually, more arrests than for any other crime except drug abuse and larceny-theft. In 1996 police made about 500,000 arrests for public drunkenness, another crime related to alcohol abuse.

Guns and Crime

In a typical year about 12,000 murders are committed in the United States with firearms—most with handguns. Handguns are used in many other crimes as well. Approximately one million serious crimes in which a handgun is used, including homicide, rape, robbery, and assault, occur each year.

Gun ownership
Over 200 million firearms are in circulation, including 70 million handguns. The production of new firearms adds two million new handguns each year to the total. Juveniles are currently more likely to carry guns than adults. Many people own guns for protection in their homes. About half the families in the United States have a gun in their homes. Because of the huge number of guns in circulation, existing gun laws are difficult to enforce.

Guns manufactured
During the past 20 years, the main type of gun made in the United States has shifted from manual revolvers to semiautomatic pistols. According to the U.S. Department of Justice, about one-third of the 223 million firearms manufactured for domestic sale or imported into the United States from 1899 through 1993 were handguns (77 million), and two-thirds were rifles (79 million) or shotguns (66 million).

Anti-gun lawsuits

During the late 1990s, many U.S. cities filed lawsuits against the gun industry. The suits charge that the gunmakers have failed to incorporate safety devices in their products or have allowed their handguns to be marketed in ways that make them easy for criminal and juveniles to buy. While the cities are seeking monetary damages in these civil lawsuits (to compensate them for excess police and hospital costs incurred by gun violence), their real purpose is to pressure gunmakers into supporting more regulation to limit the flow of handguns. The cities are using the lawsuits as a means to reduce violent crime. These lawsuits are based on new findings from the Bureau of Alcohol, Tobacco, and Firearms (ATF) that as many as half of the guns used in crimes are new guns that criminals stole.

Backed by the National Rifle Association, gun manufacturers are trying to block the lawsuits by using their allies in state legislatures to pass laws prohibiting cities from suing. Gunmakers argue that the lawsuits are nothing more than gun control in disguise. Critics of the gun industry charge that a responsible industry would concentrate on designing products with effective safety locks and on requiring dealers to limit gun purchases to one a month for each customer instead of on lobbying state legislators to pass laws exempting the gun industry from lawsuits.

Gun-control laws

The federal government and most of the states have some gun-control laws. Federal and state laws prohibit alcoholics, drug addicts, mentally unbalanced people, or people with criminal records from owning guns. Some cities require a person to buy a license to own a gun and register the serial number of the weapon with the police.

Because guns are carried across state lines, measures must be taken at the federal level to restrict the availability of firearms. The **Brady Handgun Violence Prevention Act** (1994), named for James Brady, who was shot and wounded in an attempt on President

Reagan's life in 1981, provides for a five-day waiting period before the purchase of a handgun. It also establishes a national instant criminal background checking system to be contacted by firearms dealers before the transfer of any firearm. The **Violent Crime Control and Law Enforcement Act** (1994) bans the manufacture of 19 military assault weapons.

Great Debates in Criminal Justice: Does Gun Control Reduce Crime?

It is clearly in the interests of children and families to reduce gun violence in the United States. Each day, on an average, 13 children under the age of 19 are killed by gunfire and more are injured. Homicide is the second leading cause of death for youths 10–19 years old. For black males of this age, it's the No.1 cause of death. Most youth homicides are committed with firearms, especially handguns.

A heated debate rages between those who believe in rigidly controlling guns and those who believe in no gun regulation. On one side, some gun-control advocates would like to see the government clamp down on gun manufacturers, sellers, and owners to the point that no citizens can carry guns. In general, the gun-control community wants to limit the availability of guns (which is a **supply-reduction strategy**). On the other side, the National Rifle Association (NRA) claims that the **Second Amendment** guarantees each citizen an absolute right to "bear arms." Consequently, the NRA fights all attempts to regulate the manufacture, distribution, and sale of guns. In general, the NRA and its allies favor tough sentences for criminals who use guns (which is a **demand-reduction strategy**).

Gun control does reduce crime
Gun-control advocates advance several arguments to support their position that the government should restrict the availability of guns to reduce violence.

1. More handguns in circulation equals more violent crime.

2. Owning a handgun increases a person's risk of being killed.

3. Keeping guns out of the hands of criminals prevents violent crime.

4. Taking guns away from criminals reduces violent crime.

Gun control does not reduce crime

The National Rifle Association (NRA) criticizes pro-gun-control arguments and offers an alternative proposal for reducing violence.

1. Guns don't kill—only people kill. If more people carried guns to protect themselves, there would be less violent crime.

2. Gun-control laws are unconstitutional because they violate the Second Amendment "right of the people to keep and bear arms."

3. Waiting period laws such as the Brady Bill are the first step on the road to a police state.

4. Gun control laws don't reduce violent crime.

5. An alternative to gun control—mandatory sentences for persons who commit crimes with firearms—will produce greater reductions in crime and require less sacrifice on the part of gun owners than gun-control laws.

Evaluating gun control

Proponents of gun control suggest that some of the arguments against gun control are invalid. For example, they cite statistics that support the fact that if more citizens carried guns to defend themselves, there would be little decrease in crime because crime victims rarely use weapons anyway. And they point to the fact that, so far, the U.S.

Supreme Court has refused to read the Second Amendment ("A well-regulated Militia being necessary to the security of a free State, the right of the people to keep and bear Arms, shall not be infringed") as granting a personal right to bear arms, but rather as a declaration that Congress should not do anything to displace state militias (in modern terms, the National Guard). The case most often cited is *U.S. v. Miller* (1939), which upheld a law restricting possession of a type of shotgun.

Additional refutation of anti-gun-control points involves the assertion that if more states passed mandatory sentencing laws for criminals who use guns in the commission of crimes, crime would be unaffected because in the past such laws have failed to cut crime. Gun-control advocates further point out that if more states had waiting periods and background checks, they would not usher in a police state, pointing to the fact that although Congress passed the Brady Bill in 1994, it has yet to set off a chain of further steps leading to the establishment of a police state and that there is simply no logical reason to think that waiting periods will cause the emergence of a police state.

A major question is whether or not gun-control laws reduce crime. Thus far, handgun bans have failed to have any significant impact on murder rates because of the large number of handguns in circulation prior to the bans. Attempts to outlaw the manufacture and importation of handguns have failed because they stimulate the genesis of a black market for guns similar to the black market for drugs. Laws seeking to keep handguns out of the hands of criminals, juveniles, and mental defectives have failed to reduce crime because active criminals either have guns already or can steal them. Waiting periods and background checks temporarily stop some criminals and juveniles from getting guns, but many steal them or get them through the black market.

Taking guns away from criminals is the one promising approach. Proactive arrests (made by police officers on patrols in gun-crime hot spots, using traffic enforcement and field interrogations) for carrying concealed weapons substantially reduced gun crimes in Kansas City in the mid-1990s.

An estimated 30,000 people are now in federal, state, or local prisons, primarily for violating marijuana laws. Supporters who campaign for marijuana's legalization view it as a benign recreational drug and a form of medicine, but opponents argue that marijuana promotes irresponsible sex, encourages disrespect for traditional values, and harms the user's mental, physical, and spiritual well-being. Of the thousands of criminal laws in existence in the United States, none are more controversial than the drug laws.

Sources of Criminal Law

Criminal law defines crimes; sets the procedures for arrests, searches and seizures, and interrogations; establishes the rules for trials; and specifies the punishments for offenders. Where does criminal law come from?

Common law

Common law, which is known as judge-made law, came into existence in England during the twelfth century. Judges created common law by ruling that certain actions were subject to punishment and defined offenses such as murder, rape, arson, and burglary as crimes against the state. Over time, British judges' law decisions produced a body of unwritten laws and customs. This law formed the basis of the legal system in the American colonies.

One of the main parts of common law is the **law of precedent.** Once a court makes a decision, it is binding on other courts in later cases presenting the same legal problem. The principle of *stare decisis* relates to the law of precedent. It literally means to "let the decision or precedent stand." This principle guides courts in making decisions in similar cases and ensures fairness in the judicial process.

Constitutions
Article VI of the U.S. Constitution asserts that "This Constitution . . . shall be the supreme Law of the Land; and the Judges in every State shall be bound thereby, any Thing in the Constitution or Laws of any State to the Contrary notwithstanding." If any other types of law conflict with the Constitution, the U.S. Supreme Court can strike them down as unconstitutional. States make their own constitutions and all local laws are subordinate to them.

Statutes and ordinances
Laws passed by Congress and by state legislatures make up most of criminal law. City councils also pass ordinances that compose part of criminal law. Each state has a statutory criminal code, as does the federal government. Laws defining crimes such as homicide, rape, robbery, burglary, and larceny are generally statutory. Some overlap exists between state and federal statutes. For example, some federal drug laws supplement state laws. Such laws are intended to provide added crime control in areas where local law enforcement has been ineffective.

Administrative rules with criminal penalties
U.S. governmental agencies and commissions make rules that are semilegislative or semijudicial in character. The Federal Trade Commission (FTC), Internal Revenue Service (IRS), and Environmental Protection Agency (EPA) are examples of administrative agencies that make such rules. These agencies formulate rules, investigate violations, and impose sanctions. They enforce rules relating to a variety of crimes, including securities fraud, income tax evasion, selling contaminated food, and dumping toxic waste.

Appellate court decisions
Legal opinions having the status of law as stated by the appellate courts (for example, the U.S. Supreme Court) become **case law.** Such law results from appellate court interpretations of statutory law or from court decisions where rules have not yet been codified in statutes.

The Nature of Criminal Law

To understand criminal law, it is necessary to distinguish criminal from civil law and to know the difference between substantive and procedural law.

Criminal law versus civil law
All law other than criminal law is known as **civil law.** It includes tort law (private wrongs and damages), property law, and contract law. Differences between criminal law and civil law are important because criminal proceedings are separate from civil actions. Table 1-1 shows these differences.

Table 1-1: Differences between Criminal and Civil Law

Criminal Law	*Civil Law*
Crime as public wrong	Tort as private wrong
Punishment as incarceration or death	Punishment as compensation
Government as prosecutor	Injured person as plaintiff
Proof: Beyond a reasonable doubt	Proof: Preponderance of evidence

Substantive versus procedural law

Criminal law encompasses both substantive criminal law and criminal procedure. **Substantive law** defines proscribed behaviors and specifies penalties. Laws concerning murder, rape, and robbery are substantive in that they define unlawful acts. **Procedural law** consists of rules stating how the government proceeds against an individual accused of committing a crime. Trial by jury, the right to counsel, the right to appeal, and the right to face one's accusers are just a few examples of procedural law. Violations of these rights by the government are violations of due process. If the government violates procedural law, that violation can be grounds for appeal and for a reversal of a criminal conviction.

Functions of Criminal Law

Criminal law serves several purposes and benefits society in the following ways:

- **Maintaining order.** Criminal law provides predictability, letting people know what to expect from others. Without criminal law, there would be chaos and uncertainty.

- **Resolving disputes.** The law makes it possible to resolve conflicts and disputes between quarreling citizens. It provides a peaceful, orderly way to handle grievances.

- **Protecting individuals and property.** Criminal law protects citizens from criminals who would inflict physical harm on others or take their worldly goods. Because of the importance of property in capitalist America, many criminal laws are intended to punish those who steal.

- **Providing for smooth functioning of society.** Criminal law enables the government to collect taxes, control pollution, and accomplish other socially beneficial tasks.

- **Safeguarding civil liberties.** Criminal law protects individual rights.

Legal Elements of a Crime

All crimes feature certain elements. Unless the government is able to prove the existence of these elements, it can't obtain a conviction in a court of law.

No crime without law

There can be no crime without law. If an act is to be prohibited, a legally authoritative body (such as Congress or a state legislature) must spell out in advance what behavior is banned. The U.S. Constitution forbids **ex post facto laws,** which declare certain acts to be illegal *after* the behavior occurs. The Constitution also requires that criminal laws be written in precise terms so that a citizen can determine what conduct is illegal.

No crime without a criminal act

In American criminal justice, the government punishes people for what they do rather than for what they think or say. The First Amendment protects an individual's freedom of thought and speech. The failure to act, however, can be a crime in situations in which an individual has a legal responsibility to do something. Tax laws and child-neglect laws are two examples. Threatening to act and attempting a criminal act can both be criminal offenses. Similarly, conspiring to commit a crime is illegal. Conspiracy statutes criminalize taking steps to carry out a plan to commit a crime.

No crime without intent

Intent pertains to the state of mind or mental attitude with which a person does an act. A synonym for intent, *mens rea*, literally means "guilty mind." The mental design or purpose to commit a crime is the essence of intent.

No crime without concurrence

For an act to be a crime, both the act and the intent must occur at the same time.

Legal Defenses and Justifications for Crimes

For an act to be a crime, it must be not only intentional and in violation of a criminal law, but also without defense or justification. **Defense** refers to situations that can mitigate guilt in a criminal case. Two common defenses are insanity and entrapment. **Justification** is any just cause for committing an act that otherwise would be a crime. Self-defense is a prime example.

Insanity

Insanity is a legal term, not a medical term. It refers to any unsoundness of mind, mental defect, or lack of reason that prevents people from distinguishing right from wrong and from understanding the consequences of their actions. Guilty defendants can be found "not guilty by reason of insanity" because of the belief that people should be punished for their crimes only if they could control their behavior and knew what they were doing was wrong. Otherwise, it is improper to hold people morally accountable for criminal behavior.

Courts use several tests of insanity. Under the **M'Naghten rule** (1843), defendants are considered not guilty by reason of insanity if at the time of the crime they were unable to distinguish right from wrong. All federal courts and about half of the state courts have the **Model Penal Code's substantial capacity test.** A person is not responsible for criminal conduct "if at the time of such conduct as a result of a mental disease or defect he or she lacks substantial capacity either to appreciate the criminality of his or her conduct or to conform his or her conduct to the requirements of law." This test provides a broader, more encompassing definition of insanity than the M'Naghten rule. Defendants pleading insanity under the substantial capacity test have to show only that they are mostly unable to function mentally.

The **Comprehensive Crime Control Act** (1984) changed the federal rules on the insanity defense, limiting it to those who are unable to understand the wrongfulness of their acts as a result of severe mental disease. This act shifted the burden of proof to the defense. Now, the defense must prove beyond a reasonable doubt that the defendant was insane at the time of the crime. Under this law, a person who is found not guilty only by reason of insanity must be committed to a mental hospital until he or she no longer poses a threat to society. Many state courts have adopted these rules.

A common misperception about the insanity defense is that it allows many violent criminals to escape punishment for their acts. Studies show that the insanity plea is used in fewer than one percent of serious criminal cases and is rarely successful. When it succeeds, offenders generally spend more time in mental institutions than they would have spent in prison if they had been convicted.

Entrapment
Entrapment is a legal defense that sets free the suspect who has been induced by law enforcement agents to commit a crime. The U.S. Supreme Court invented the entrapment doctrine to control outrageous, overreaching police activity that endangers civil liberties and

violates fundamental fairness. The Court's **subjective test,** which most state courts and all federal courts follow, holds that entrapment occurs when a law enforcement agent puts a criminal idea into the mind of an innocent person who otherwise would not have committed the offense. The focus is on the predisposition of the defendant: Did the idea to commit the crime originate with the defendant or law enforcement?

Self-defense

A person defending himself or herself can use only **reasonable force** in self-defense. How much force is reasonable depends on the circumstances of each situation. The force used to repel an attack should be proportionate to the amount of force used against the defendant. To use this defense, the danger must be imminent and the defendant must look for alternative ways of avoiding the danger. The rules of self-defense also apply to defense of another and the defense of property. Defendants can support a self-defense argument with evidence that a victim had a history of violence, and the prosecution can produce evidence that the victim was not prone to violence. Some states also allow the prosecution to offer evidence of the defendant's history of violence.

The Limits of Criminal Law

Amidst the war on drugs of the 1980s, Congress passed legislation authorizing federal prosecutors to go after drug dealers and drug kingpins. Next came carjackers, arsonists, deadbeat dads and moms who flee from their duty to pay child support, and bigots who commit hate crimes. The rationale for expanding federal criminal law into these areas is that local police forces have been ineffective in controlling certain kinds of crime. Chief Justice Rehnquist complained in 1999 that Congress is contributing to rising caseloads in federal courts by federalizing crimes already covered by state laws.

Is the act of passing laws a viable solution to the crime problem in the United States? Criminologist Nigel Walker argues there are limits to what criminal law can do and proposes several rules that legislators can use when deciding whether to criminalize certain behaviors.

Legislators should not use criminal law to penalize harmless behavior

Most people in the United States would agree with Walker's idea that harmless behavior should not be penalized, but many would disagree about what is harmful. Then, too, there is the question of "harmful to whom?" Walker and many other liberals think that legislators should criminalize only behavior that is harmful to others. By contrast, conservatives are generally in favor of passing laws that keep citizens from hurting themselves and others.

Legislators should not use criminal law if the penalty does more harm than the offense

On June 8, 1998, the *New York Times* published an open letter to the United Nations Secretary General as the General Assembly opened a special session on drugs. The letter declared that the global war on drugs has cost society more than drug abuse itself. The letter stated that by focusing on punishing drug users, the United States has created a world-wide criminal black market that is wrecking national economies and democratic governments. Despite the letter's assertion comparing the costs of drug criminalization versus drug abuse, the letter failed to provide any estimates of the costs of drug abuse.

Legislators should not include in criminal law prohibitions that the public does not support

Walker suggests that legislators shouldn't outlaw something that lots of people want. Take, for example, the U.S. government's criminalization of narcotic drugs. Many Americans want these drugs for recreational and medicinal purposes. Or consider the failure of states that have attempted to ban physician-assisted suicide. Many Americans believe that helping people into death is not abandonment, but rather compassionate care.

Legislators should not use criminal law to condemn wicked acts

Walker takes issue with ultraconservative politicians and religious leaders who try to legislate morality. To assert moral sentiments for a new criminal law, Walker says, invites an argument as to what is or is not wicked. In a society as diverse as that of the United States, it is easy to find areas of disagreement about good and evil.

Great Debates in Criminal Justice: Should Drugs Be Legalized?

Policymakers in the United States have chosen to define drug abuse as a legal problem rather than a public-health problem. This choice puts the criminal justice system at the center of a massive war on drugs. The drug war is an expanding enterprise with deep roots in the political and social fabric of the U.S. society. It is an effort that involves law enforcement, courts, corrections, education, health care, and a multitude of political groups. Started by the Reagan administration and expanded by the Bush and Clinton administrations, the drug war depicts the U.S. as fighting a deadly enemy. The term **drug war** refers to a situation created when the government puts its power behind the drug laws, zealously enforces them, and imprisons large numbers of drug offenders as if they were enemies in a real war.

The main solutions to the drug problem focus on supply and demand. **Supply-side solutions** include initiatives aimed at pressuring drug-producing countries to halt the exporting of illegal drugs, intercepting drugs before smugglers can get them across American borders, passing tougher drug laws, cracking down on drug dealers, and sentencing drug manufacturers and dealers to long prison terms. **Demand-side solutions** include drug education and drug treatment. A more radical approach suggests **legalization** (in other words, removal of drug offense from criminal codes) as the only viable solution.

Drugs should be legalized
There are numerous arguments for drug legalization.

1. Criminal prohibition of drugs has not eliminated or substantially reduced drug use.

2. The drug war has cost society more than drug abuse itself. Costs include the $16 billion the federal government alone spent to fight drugs in 1998. Of this $16 billion, $10.5 billion pays for measures to reduce the supply of drugs. Most of these measures involve law enforcement efforts to interdict or intercept drug supplies at the borders. Costs also include corruption, damage to poor and minority neighborhoods, a world-wide black market in illegal drugs, the enrichment of criminal organizations through their involvement in the drug trade, and an increase in predatory crimes, such as robberies and burglaries, committed by drug addicts who are enslaved to drugs.

3. Most illegal drugs are no more harmful than legal substances, such as cigarettes and alcohol, and therefore, drugs should be treated the same as these other substances.

4. Legalization would free up billions of dollars that the government now spends on police, courts, and corrections to wage war on drugs and would produce significant tax revenues. The money saved could then be spent on drug education, drug treatment, and law enforcement initiatives directed at more serious crimes.

5. Drug prohibition infringes on civil liberties. The U.S. Supreme Court has decided that because drugs are such a horrible thing, it is okay to bend the Fourth Amendment (which relates to searches and seizures) in order to make it easier to secure convictions in drug cases.

Drugs should not be legalized

There are also many arguments against legalization.

1. Legalization would increase the number of casual users which, in turn, would increase the number of drug abusers.

2. More drug users, abusers, and addicts would mean more health problems and lower economic productivity.

3. Although legalization might result in savings in expensive criminal justice costs and provide tax revenues, increased public-health costs and reduced economic productivity due to more drug-dependent workers would offset the financial benefits of legalization.

4. The argument based on the analogy between alcohol and tobacco versus psychoactive drugs is weak because its conclusion—psychoactive drugs should be legalized—does not follow from its premises. It is illogical to say that because alcohol and tobacco take a terrible toll (for example, they are responsible for 500,000 premature deaths each year), a heavy toll from legalization is therefore acceptable. Indeed, the reverse seems more logical: prohibit the use of alcohol, tobacco, and psychoactive drugs because of the harm they all do. Additionally, marijuana, heroin, cocaine, crack, and the rest of the psychoactive drugs are not harmless substances—they have serious negative consequences for the health of users and addictive liability.

Evaluating drug legalization

Is legalization a gamble worth taking? Arguments on both sides are persuasive. What should we do if we can neither clearly accept nor reject drug legalization? One approach proposed as being sensible is to suspend judgment, to recognize that proponents of legalization are partly right (that the drug war has proven ineffective in reducing drug abuse and crime associated with drugs), and to realize that it is time to explore new approaches.

CHAPTER 5
DEVELOPMENT OF THE AMERICAN POLICE

Knowing the history of the police in the United States is of critical importance in understanding the police today. Samuel Walker, a noted criminal justice scholar, argues that the historical perspective allows one to see how and why changes have taken place in police systems. The study of police history also reveals what the origins of current police problems are and why they are so hard to solve.

Policing Colonial America

Many European law enforcement institutions were transplanted in the colonies.

The county sheriff

The most important law enforcement official in colonial America was the county sheriff. The sheriff was responsible for enforcing the laws, collecting taxes, supervising elections, and taking care of the legal business of the county government. The sheriff job was **reactive**—after a citizen filed a complaint or provided information about a crime, the sheriff would initiate an investigation or arrest a suspect. The sheriff did not patrol areas or take other actions that might prevent crime.

Fragmentation of law enforcement authority

Villages and cities added other law enforcement authorities. In New York City, for example, the mayor, constable, police justices, marshals, and night watch all had some responsibility for protecting the city. The **mayor** was the chief law enforcement officer, whose law enforcement duty consisted of taking charge of the protection of the city during riots. The mayor hired constables and marshals as

assistants. **Constables** and **marshals** had law enforcement powers similar to the sheriff's. They could make arrests, serve warrants, and testify in court. The **night watch** consisted of a group of citizens who patrolled the city at night, looking for fires, crimes, or riots. The night watch served during the night, while the constables and marshals were the main law enforcement officials on duty during the day. Eventually, cities added the **day watch.** Whenever riots broke out, colonial authorities called out the **militia.**

Benefits and costs of fragmentation

The wide distribution of police authority in colonial times still exists in the United States today. Whereas many countries in the world have a national police force, police power in the U.S. has always been decentralized. Just as citizens in colonial America would have viewed such a centralized police force with deep suspicion, Americans today would fear that a national police might be misused by a leader seeking to set up an authoritarian regime. The decentralization of police authority, which began in colonial America, is a safeguard against the subversion of democracy.

Although it has benefits, the fragmentation of law enforcement authority also carries costs. The multiplicity of policing agencies at various levels of government results in duplication of effort and wasted resources. Fragmentation remains an obstacle to efficient law enforcement today.

Developing the New Police

The period between the end of the Revolutionary War and 1900 was a time of disorder and change in this country. Industrialization, urbanization, immigration, and slavery contributed to crime and disorder. Seeking a new mechanism for social control, Americans borrowed the London model of policing.

Robert Peel and the "Bobbies"

Robert Peel, a politician, convinced British Parliament to pass the Metropolitan Police Act in 1829. It abolished the night watch in England and established a full-time, uniformed police force whose primary purpose was preventing crime and disorder. Under Peel's leadership, the London police introduced new elements into law enforcement. Instead of watching for crime or waiting for a night watchman "to raise the hue and cry," the London police set **crime prevention** as their goal. The mission of this publicly funded force was **proactive**—it tried to prevent crime before it occurred. To accomplish this goal, the London police embraced **preventive patrol.** Police administrators had **Bobbies** (a nickname for London police derived from Peel's first name) walking **beats** (areas of the city). It was assumed that the presence of Bobbies on the streets would deter would-be criminals from breaking the law. Peel also instituted a **military style of administration.** Officers had ranks, wore uniforms, and adhered to an authoritarian system of command and discipline.

Adopting the London model

Americans selectively incorporated parts of the London model. They adopted the approach of crime prevention through patrol and organized police agencies along military lines. But the London Metropolitan Police were too elitist for Americans. Whereas the British made their new police an agency of the national government, Americans opted for a more democratic police. Americans were given a much more direct voice in police administration than the British. Power and authority were highly centralized in the London police, and the police department was insulated from political influence. Unlike the London police, American police departments were decentralized with political leaders in wards and neighborhoods exerting power over police recruitment, policies, and practices.

The first American police department

Boston's day watch, which was created in 1838, ranks as the first modern-style police force in the United States. New York City formed its police department in 1844. The foundation for today's modern police was laid in these departments. In most cities, the creation of a modern police force meant adding a day watch or combining the day and night watches. Employing officers on a full-time basis and paying them salaries were other important steps.

The problem of political control

Political machines ruled the cities and controlled the police. Machine politicians in a particular city doled out police jobs to members of ethnic groups for political support. Such political patronage produced a police force that reflected the racial/ethnic makeup of the machine's political constituents.

The problem of corruption

Corruption was pervasive. The police ignored vice laws (in other words, laws regulating drinking, prostitution, and gambling) in return for payoffs from vice entrepreneurs. Efforts to stamp out police corruption failed because politically powerful groups benefited from it.

The problem of police brutality and racial/ethnic discrimination

Longstanding conflicts between the police and the public created tension between them. The public regarded the untrained, unsupervised police as nothing more than political hacks. Americans believed the adoption of the police institution was too authoritarian for a democratic society. Police brutality often occurred within a context of racial and class conflict.

Frontier Justice

The absence of any law enforcement authority in the western territories was a major problem. A variety of private and public police filled the void.

- **Vigilantes.** Vigilante committees were made up of citizens who arrested, tried, convicted, and punished individuals.

- **Sheriffs.** The first formal law enforcement agency to emerge in the territories beyond the Mississippi was the sheriff's office.

- **State police.** The first territorial police agency established in the United States was the Texas Rangers. Originally, the Rangers were a corps of fighters who fought in the Texas revolution against Mexico in 1835. Later, the Rangers evolved into a law enforcement agency. Pennsylvania formed the first modern state police in 1905. Within the next 20 years, state police became common. For the most part, early state police broke up labor strikes and performed other duties that local police were unwilling or unable to do.

- **U.S. Marshals.** Federal marshals constituted the oldest federal law enforcement agency, established in 1789. In the 19th century, horseback-riding marshals made arrests, served court papers, managed federal prisoners, and conducted the U.S. population census.

Progressive Police Reform

At the end of the 19th century, progressives attempted to reform the police. **Progressivism** was a social movement advocating progress, change, improvement, and reform as opposed to maintaining things as they were. Reacting to the demands of an urban-industrial society in the early 1900s, Progressives advanced the ideas of regulating corporations, eliminating corruption from municipal government, abolishing child labor, and extending the right to vote to women. Under the leadership of Theodore Roosevelt (who later served as the 26th president from 1901 to 1909), a small group of eastern **civilian reformers** entered municipal government, made important contributions to police administration, and moved on to careers in other fields. As president of the New York City Board of Police Commissioners (1895–1897), Roosevelt advocated reforms designed to reduce the power of political machines over the police.

Civil service

Civilian reformers instituted civil service. Under civil service, appointments and status are determined by merit and examination rather than by political patronage. Eventually, civil service helped to get rid of political patronage in American police departments.

Other recommended changes

Civilian reformers recommended these other changes:

1. Centralizing power and authority within police departments.

2. Upgrading police personnel.

3. Narrowing the police function so that police could focus on law enforcement aspects of policing.

4. Eliminating politics from policing.

Police as social workers

Some progressives saw the police as social workers. To implement the social work role, a few police departments hired women officers. When the Portland Police Department hired Lola Baldwin for child protection duty at the World's Fair in Portland in 1905, she became the first woman police officer in the United States. Alice Stebbins Wells, a policewoman with the Los Angeles Police Department, stressed the idea that policewomen should play a helping role similar to that of the mother in the home. This sex-role stereotyping relegated women to work with juveniles and barred them from patrol until the latter part of the 20th century.

Police Professionalism

Progressive thinking about how to improve the police paved the way for a second reform movement. Within police circles, a group of police chiefs advocated professionalizing the police. The professional police department was administratively efficient, organizationally separate from political influences, technologically advanced, and expertly staffed.

August Vollmer

Following the lead of the progressives, August Vollmer, the chief of police in Berkeley, California, from 1909–1932, championed police professionalism. Vollmer defined police professionalism in terms of efficient crime control, nonpartisanship, college-educated police officers, and public service. Vollmer is known for many firsts. He was the first to develop an academic degree program in law enforcement. His police agency, the Berkeley (California) Police Department, was the first to use forensic science in solving crimes and the first to use automobiles. His agency was also one of the first to create what is now called a code of ethics, which introduced prohibitions against the acceptance of gratuities, rewards, or favors.

O. W. Wilson

Vollmer's student O. W. Wilson emphasized the application of scientific management principles to police bureaucracy to increase efficiency. As chief of police in Wichita, Kansas, Wilson was one of the

first to favor single-officer patrol cars. As a professor at the University of California at Berkeley, Wilson became the nation's top expert on police administration.

Crime Control Decades (1919–1959)

While Vollmer and Wilson were laying out the professional model of policing, crime control became the central concern of law enforcement.

The Red Scare

The Red Scare of 1919–1920 consisted of the federal government's, state governments', and vigilantes' suppressing of dissent by radical and left-wing groups. It reached a climax with the **Palmer raids** in January 1920. U.S. Attorney General A. Mitchell Palmer orchestrated a series of raids that produced thousands of arrests in 33 cities. The **Bureau of Investigation,** a federal agency established in 1908, compiled a list of subversives prior to the raids and fostered the fiction that citizens who dissented from government policies were disloyal.

Riots and police racism

More than 20 race riots broke out in the summer of 1919. Studies of these riots reveal discriminatory law enforcement and police participation in the riots.

Expansion of the federal role in law enforcement

Passage of the Harrison Act (1914) and the Volstead Act (1919) expanded the scope of federal jurisdiction over criminal activity. The **Harrison Act** required physicians marketing drugs to register with the government and pay taxes. To enforce the federal government's

first drug law, Congress created the **Drug Enforcement Administration.** The **Volstead Ac**t banned the manufacture, distribution, and sale of alcoholic beverages. To enforce the dry law, Congress established the **Bureau of Prohibition** (which was a forerunner of the Bureau of Alcohol, Tobacco, and Firearms, a branch of the Treasury Department). Both drug prohibition laws had the unintended consequences of providing an impetus for the growth of organized crime and causing epidemics of police corruption. Pressure on the police to do something to enforce these unpopular, unenforceable laws encouraged the police to violate the civil liberties of many citizens.

J. Edgar Hoover and the Federal Bureau of Investigation (FBI)
J. Edgar Hoover, who served as FBI director from 1924–1972, was the most famous and controversial figure to appear in 20th-century law enforcement. During the 1930s, Hoover's FBI agents tracked down and captured such gangsters as "Baby Face" Nelson, John Dillinger, "Pretty Boy" Floyd, "Ma" Barker, and the bank robbers/murderers Bonnie Parker and Clyde Barrow. Under Hoover's direction, the FBI became a standard-setter for law enforcement in the U.S. and the leading example of police professionalism. Hoover's idea of police professionalism included an emphasis on efficient crime-fighting, police training, scientific crime detection (for example, fingerprinting and lie detecting), a stress on firearms, an authoritarian style of management, and a cynical attitude toward the Constitution in which police officers were to avoid violating citizens' rights not because it was the right thing to do, but because it might result in the loss of a case on appeal. This evangelist for crime control eventually went too far when he attempted to repress political dissent during the Vietnam War and the struggle for civil rights in the 1960s.

Technological and administrative changes
During the 1900s, automobiles, telephones, and radios all enhanced the crime-fighting capabilities of the American police. Police agencies converted from foot to motorized patrol, allowed citizens' telephone

calls for assistance to drive police activities, and used the radio to tighten up monitoring of officers on the streets. Some of these technological innovations had unintended effects on the police. For example, the patrol car removed the officer from the street and reduced police-citizen contacts, isolating the police from the communities they were responsible for policing.

Policing the Social Crises of the 1960s

During the turbulent 1960s, a variety of social and legal forces renewed interest in police reform.

Racism and the police

To many residents living in the U.S. in the 1960s, the police symbolized a society that denied black citizens equal justice. Police actions ignited race riots in almost every city in the United States. The National Advisory Commission on Civil Disorders (the **Kerner Commission,** named after its chairperson, Otto Kerner) blamed the riots on racism. It stated that "our nation is moving toward two societies, one black, one white—separate and unequal." The Kerner Commission criticized law enforcement for the underrepresentation of blacks on police forces, brutality and abuse of power, and racial bias in the use of deadly force.

Police departments responded in several ways. First, they started **police-community relations programs** to improve communication between the police and racial minority citizens. Second, departments initiated **affirmative action programs** to recruit and promote more blacks and women. Third, some big city police departments formulated **written policies for the use of deadly force** to reduce racial disparities in police shootings.

The due process revolution and the police

The Warren Court handed down a series of decisions between 1961 and 1969 that expanded citizens' due process rights and limited police powers. Some police administrators complained that Fourth and Fifth Amendment limits on police powers to question, arrest, search, and seize made it impossible for the police to fight crime. Civil liberties advocates heralded the revolution in criminal procedure as a way to ensure that the police treated those accused of crimes fairly.

Street crime and the federalization of law enforcement

Between 1960 and 1974, index crimes skyrocketed nationally from 3,363,700 to over 10 million per year. In addition to the upward spiral in crime, drug abuse spread from the ghettos to the white middle class. The federal government responded by passing crime control legislation and by creating the **Law Enforcement Assistance Administration (LEAA).** LEAA served as a conduit through which the federal government funneled millions of dollars into state and local police agencies. LEAA's **Law Enforcement Education Program** (LEEP) helped thousands of officers pay for a college education. LEAA money assisted in the development of hundreds of criminal justice programs in colleges and universities across the nation. Technological innovations, such as computers and modern communications devices, changed the ways in which police kept records and communicated with one another.

The resurgence of police unionism

Employment conditions in police departments worsened, and rank-and-file officers became alienated by the due process revolution. These developments led to an outburst of police unionism. Strikes of police became common in big cities. Unions won improvements in salaries and benefits for officers along with protections for them in disciplinary hearings. There was a redistribution of power within police departments. Police unions reduced the power of police administrators, who now are forced to consult with union officials over management issues.

Crime Control Revisited (1970s–1990s)

As the political mood of the country turned conservative during the 1970s, 1980s, and 1990s, crime control dominated the police agenda in the United States.

Controlling street crime

American police experimented with a variety of programs designed to control street crime. Scientific evaluations show that these police programs reduce crime:

1. Extra police patrols in high-crime hot spots.

2. Repeat offender units that monitor repeat offenders on the streets.

3. Efforts to arrest employed suspects who engage in domestic abuse (studies indicate that arrests are more likely to deter employed spouse abusers than unemployed abusers).

Other police programs do *not* work. These include neighborhood watch programs, which fail to reduce burglaries, and police crackdowns on drug markets, which fail to reduce violent crime or disorder for more than a few days.

Controlling illegal drugs

Controlling drugs and fighting drug-related crime are among the major responsibilities of law enforcement at all levels of government. Police involvement in the drug war is costly. First, economic costs are staggering. For example, federal expenditures for drug control rose from $1.5 billion in 1981 to $18 billion in 1998. Drug-related law enforcement consumes more than half of this budget. Treatment, education, crop control, **interdiction** (interception of drugs), research, and intelligence account for the rest. Second, police involvement in the drug war exacerbates police corruption. Of course,

police corruption is nothing new. Police corruption related to liquor laws when alcohol prohibition was in effect. The same type of prohibition-style corruption is rampant in drug enforcement today. More than 100 drug corruption cases involving law enforcement officers are prosecuted in federal and state courts each year. Third, the drug war poisons police-community relations. Some lawyers, activists, and politicians claim the drug war is racist. As proof of police racism, they assert that in some cities the main targets in the war on drugs are minority neighborhoods and minority suspects. Fourth, strict enforcement of the drug laws may actually make the drug problem worse by boosting drug prices and by increasing profits for drug traffickers.

Police drug-education programs have not fared much better than the law enforcement programs. During the 1990s, thousands of school districts across America involved the police teaching DARE (Drug Abuse Resistance Education). Recent evaluations show DARE does not prevent students from using illegal drugs.

The déjà vu character of police brutality
Just as police brutality reared its ugly head in the first big city police departments in the 19th century, it resurfaced in many U.S. cities during the 1990s. After the Rodney King incident, the National Association for the Advancement of Colored People held hearings in six cities on the issue of police brutality of minorities. A report written by the Criminal Justice Institute at Harvard Law School documents examples of excessive force, verbal abuse, unjustified searches, and trumped-up charges against minorities. Critics rhetorically pose the question "Who will police the police?"

The crime control counterrevolution
In response to the issue of controlling the police, the Burger Supreme Court (1969–1986) and the Rehnquist Court (1986–) have deferred to the police to control themselves. The appointment of new justices by conservative Republican presidents and others by a middle-of-the-road Democratic president swung the makeup of the Supreme Court to the right. Under the leadership of Warren Burger and William

Rehnquist, the Court has carved out exceptions to the due process rights established by the liberal Warren Court. The net effect of rulings by the conservative Burger and Rehnquist Courts on criminal procedure has been to unshackle the police from Fourth and Fifth Amendment limitations.

Law Enforcement Goes High-Tech

At the beginning of the 21st century, modern technology is revolutionizing crime-fighting. Some devices make police officers more productive and improve their safety.

Advanced microphones

The FBI's research lab is producing microminiature electronic surveillance equipment customized for each investigation. The FBI has developed, for example, a solid-state, briefcase-size, electronically steerable microphone that can monitor conversations across open areas.

Closed circuit television cameras (CCTC)

The FBI has miniature CCTC units its agents can put in a lamp, clock radio, briefcase, duffel bag, purse, picture frame, coin telephone, book, and other objects and then control remotely to pan, tilt, zoom, and focus.

Forward-looking infrared (FLIR)

Law enforcement agents can point heat detectors at neighborhoods to detect higher temperatures in houses where artificial lights are used to grow marijuana.

Intelligent transportation systems (ITS)

Traffic management technologies, including crash-avoidance systems, automated toll collection, and satellite-based position location, can be used to track the movement of all people using private or public transportation and the movement of people using cellular phones. In 1993, fugitive Colombian drug kingpin Pablo Escobar was pinpointed through his cellular phone.

Databases

The FBI's **National Crime Information Center (NCIC)** contains over 24 million records and connects over 500,000 users in 19,000 federal, state, and local agencies. Every year, law enforcement agents access over a million NCIC records for criminal investigations.

DNA typing

DNA typing played a central role in the murder case against former pro football player O. J. Simpson. DNA typing saves police time and money by quickly eliminating large numbers of potential suspects. DNA, or deoxyribonucleic acid, is contained in all the body's cells. It carries the genetic codes that are believed to control the body's physical traits, such as race, hair, and eye color. Scientists believe that no two people, other than identical twins, have identical DNA. Sperm and blood cells are particularly rich in DNA, making DNA testing a useful tool in murder and rape cases. Capitalizing on this technological breakthrough in crime-fighting, the FBI opened a national DNA database in 1998. It consists of 50 databases run by the states but unified by common test procedures and software designed by the FBI. It is now possible to compare a DNA sample from a suspect or crime scene in one state with all others in the system.

Great Debates in Criminal Justice: Should Police Take DNA
Samples from *All* Arrestees?

Under some state laws, a state collects DNA samples from people
who have been convicted of major crimes, such as rape and homicide.
Prosecutors can also get a court order to take blood and DNA samples if they have probable cause to target an individual in an investigation. New York's police commissioner proposed in 1998 to collect
DNA samples from everyone arrested in New York City.

Police should take DNA samples from all arrestees
Some support the extension of this ultrapowerful form of tracking to
all arrestees on the grounds of better crime control. Proponents of
such DNA sampling make the following arguments:

1. DNA sampling, done by collecting saliva, poses no danger
   to civil liberties because it is pretty much the same as taking
   fingerprints.

2. Taking samples of DNA from all arrestees would dramatically
   improve law enforcement's efficiency and effectiveness in solving crimes and in exonerating innocent persons. Thousands of
   people have been convicted because suspects can be searched
   out across space and time based on DNA evidence. Hundreds
   of innocent people have also been freed, often after years behind
   bars, sometimes just short of the death penalty.

Police should not take DNA samples from all arrestees
Civil libertarians see grave dangers in the mass DNA testing of all
arrestees and put forth these arguments in support of their position.

1. Expanding the scope of DNA typing to include all arrestees rather than just felons would make it likely that such typing would eventually be broadened to include everyone. This argument is based on the premise that the insurance industry, corporate employers, politicians, and government bureaucrats will press for mass DNA typing for their own benefits or the good of society.

2. The analogical argument comparing fingerprints to DNA is flawed. Whereas fingerprints can't be used for any purpose other than identification, DNA samples can be misused in a variety of ways. The threat of genetic discrimination based on DNA banking is real. Genetic discrimination is the use of genetic information derived from tests to classify individuals on the basis of their genetic status and to discriminate against those at risk for future health problems. For example, insurance companies could use DNA data to identify those at risk for genetic disease and refuse coverage to at-risk individuals.

3. Barry Scheck, a professor at Yeshiva University's Cardozo School of Law in Greenwich Village, heads the Innocence Project, which uses DNA evidence to try to clear wrongly convicted clients. Scheck, the DNA expert on O. J. Simpson's "dream team" of lawyers, argues that "using DNA data banks effectively does not require taking samples from all citizens, as some rightly fear, or even expanding the data bank beyond felony offenders." According to Scheck, "We don't need to test more people; we need more labs testing more crime scenes." In other words, the problem is that DNA laboratories in the United States are so underfunded they can't type enough cases. He says DNA labs are so backlogged it often takes ten months to get results in a case in which a suspect has already been apprehended and is awaiting trial.

4. The civil liberties costs (including the invasion of the genetic privacy of hundreds of thousands of citizens) of taking DNA samples from all arrestees would outweigh any social benefits to be derived from such a program.

5. Because DNA testing is very economically costly, it would not be cost-effective to take samples from persons arrested for misdemeanors and other minor offenses.

Evaluating the expansion of DNA banking to include all arrestees
Harvard law professor Lawrence Tribe notes that the U.S. Supreme Court usually fails to protect constitutional rights when dealing with new technologies. Given the crime control orientation of the current Court, Tribe is doubtful that the Court will shield the right of privacy in cases involving DNA typing. Nevertheless, it remains to be seen whether DNA typing will be extended to all arrestees. Should mass police sampling of all arrestees be prohibited to protect the genetic privacy of all individuals? Should DNA sampling be conducted only for the purpose of identifying individual criminal suspects? Because police agencies, other government bureaucracies, and corporations have misused technological inventions in the past to overstep the boundaries of individual privacy, it would seem important for Americans to be vigilant in protecting their civil liberties when it comes to DNA typing.

The myth of police as crime-fighters has been conveyed to the American people through television dramas, comic strips, and newspaper articles. It conjures up in one's mind an image of a police officer doing a dangerous job that requires him or her to outshoot, outpunch, and outwit dangerous criminals. For most American police, there is little correspondence between this image and reality. In a major metropolitan area (where crime rates are the highest), half of the officers in the local department will not make a felony arrest during a given year. The total annual rate of weapon discharges per hundred police officers is in the range of two to six.

The Nature of Police Work

What do the police really do?

Three functions

Even though we refer to the police as law enforcement officers, the enforcement of criminal law (in other words, investigating crime and apprehending criminals) is only one of several functions that the police perform. The functions of the American police include providing basic social services, maintaining order, and controlling crime.

- In the area of **social service,** the police help people who need emergency assistance, whether it is giving first aid or finding lost children. Typically, over 50 percent of the telephone calls to the police requesting assistance involve social service as compared with less than 20 percent relating to crime.

- Among the **order-maintenance** activities are traffic control, crowd control, resolving domestic disputes, and moving prostitutes from the streets. The focus of order maintenance is on handling situations to preserve the peace rather than enforcing the letter of the law. The appropriate order-maintenance solution may be making an arrest (for example, in case of domestic violence), but it often consists of some less formal action (for example, getting an illegal panhandler to move on).

- In the area of **crime control,** the police engage in a range of activities, such as patrol and criminal investigation.

Major responsibilities

The American Bar Association's *Standards Relating to the Urban Police Function* lists these 11 responsibilities:

- To identify criminal offenders and criminal activity and, when appropriate, to apprehend offenders and participate in later court proceedings.

- To reduce the opportunities for the commission of some crimes through preventive patrol and other measures.

- To aid individuals who are in danger of physical harm.

- To protect constitutional guarantees.

- To facilitate the movement of people and vehicles.

- To assist those who cannot care for themselves.

- To resolve conflict.

- To identify problems that are potentially serious law enforcement or government problems.

- To create and maintain a feeling of security in the community.

- To promote and preserve civil order.

- To provide other services on an emergency basis.

Factors shaping police work

Several factors shape what the police do. **Twenty-four hour availability** broadens police contacts with the public. People call the police because there is no other agency available. A disadvantage is that such availability gives police a heavy workload. The **authority to use force** stamps police work with a uniqueness that sets it apart from other lines of work. Force includes the right to use deadly force, to arrest people, and to use physical force. Whatever aspect of the police mission is emphasized—whether it involves checking on suspicious persons who appear to be out of place or responding to reports of crime—the police have to be willing, in the last analysis, to threaten force and to back up the threat with action. **Discretion** leaves an imprint on all areas of policing. Police are often free to choose among alternative courses of action or inaction. They routinely rely on their own experience, training, common sense, and judgment to make decisions involving the life and liberty of citizens. Examples of discretionary decision making include decisions involving arrests, traffic tickets, deadly force, and domestic abuse. In each of these situations, officers determine whether or not to invoke the power of the law.

Factors influencing discretionary decisions

The **seriousness of the crime** and the **strength of the evidence** affect an officer's decision to arrest. The more serious the crime and the stronger the evidence, the more likely an officer is to make an arrest. A **suspect's demeanor** also makes a difference. The more disrespectful and the less deferent a suspect acts toward an officer, the more likely that officer is to use force.

Police Systems

The 17,500 police agencies at national, state, county, and municipal levels employ more than 800,000 people, sworn and unsworn. The agencies include

- 50 federal law enforcement agencies.
- 49 state police departments.
- 1,721 special police agencies (for example, transit police and school police).
- 3,086 sheriff's departments.
- 12,502 municipal police departments.

Federal police agencies

Federal law enforcement agencies are part of the executive branch of the national government. The major federal law enforcement agencies are

- **The Federal Bureau of Investigation (FBI):** This Department of Justice (DOJ) agency investigates over 200 categories of federal crimes. The FBI emphasizes protecting the nation from terrorism, organized crime (which includes narcotics trafficking), white-collar crimes, civil-rights crimes, and violent crimes (such as bank robbery and kidnapping). It assists other federal, state, and local agencies through its crime statistics, crime lab, fingerprint files, and training academy. As organized crime has become a bigger business, the FBI has gained additional authority (including wiretapping authority) to combat it.

- **The Bureau of Alcohol, Tobacco, and Firearms (ATF):** This Treasury Department agency investigates the criminal use of explosives and firearms. ATF also pursues outlaw motorcycle gangs who violate federal firearms, explosives, and drug trafficking laws.

- **The Drug Enforcement Administration (DEA):** This DOJ agency is responsible for enforcing all federal drug-control laws. Its agents investigate narcotics violators, seize drugs, and arrest drug traffickers.

- **The U.S. Marshals Service:** Today's marshals provide security for all federal courts. They also protect members of the federal judiciary, except for the U.S. Supreme Court, which has its own police force. Marshals apprehend escaped federal prisoners, supervise those arrested, and operate the federal witness protection program (which gives new identities and security to some witnesses in federal trials).

- **The Secret Service:** The Secret Service is responsible for apprehending anyone counterfeiting U.S. money and for protecting the president and other officials of the federal government.

- **The Immigration and Naturalization Service (INS):** The INS polices the flow of immigrants into the United States. INS agents patrol the U.S. border to stop illegal immigrants from entering the country, and the agency deports aliens who break U.S. naturalization laws. In the 1990s, INS agents focused on the Mexican-U.S. border, where large numbers of illegal immigrants and huge amounts of illicit drugs entered the United States. INS agents arrested hundreds of thousands of illegal immigrants each year, but the number making it safely into the United States still exceeded the number arrested.

Internationalization of law enforcement

Federal law enforcement agencies are increasingly stationing officers overseas. This trend is a response to the global scope of such crimes as drug trafficking, money laundering, and terrorism. By 1998, more than 1,500 American law enforcement officers were assigned to more than 50 countries.

State police

Every state except Hawaii has its own police force with statewide jurisdiction. The California Highway Patrol is the nation's largest state police force. Governors appoint the directors of state police or highway patrols. State police agencies do some or all of the following tasks:

- Assist local law enforcement organizations in criminal investigations.

- Maintain centralized crime records for the state.

- Patrol the state's highways.

- Operate a crime lab.

- Train municipal and county police.

County police

Sheriffs are responsible for policing rural and unincorporated areas of the more than 3,000 counties in the United States. The position of county sheriff is an elected one. Many sheriffs perform law enforcement, court, and correctional duties. In many states, sheriffs operate the county jails and serve as officers of the county courts. The sheriff's office supplies bailiffs to provide security and management of defendants on trial. Sheriffs also transport prisoners to and from court and serve court papers. Sheriff's offices vary in size. The largest is the Los Angeles Sheriff's Department, with more than 11,000 full-time employees. Of the more than 3,000 sheriff's departments in the United States, 19 departments have only one employee.

Municipal police

City police represent the largest number of agencies, employ most of the sworn officers, and shoulder the heaviest responsibility for dealing with violent crime. Mayors or city managers appoint the **chiefs** that head big-city police departments. Departments vary in size and in the type of crime that faces them. The "Big Six" departments—New York, Los Angeles, Chicago, Houston, Philadelphia, and Detroit—deal with most serious violent crimes. The New York Police Department employs more than 36,000 full-time officers. It confronts shootings, scandals, and corruption that make the national headlines. Most departments employ only a few people. In small departments, most calls to the police involve traffic violations and minor disturbances.

Police Organization

The typical American police department is a bureaucracy, with a military style of operation.

The police bureaucracy
Police agencies have a bureaucratic structure. The systematic administration of police departments is characterized by specialization of tasks and duties, objective qualifications for positions, action according to rules and regulations, and a hierarchy of authority. Bureaucratization maximizes efficiency. The downside of bureaucracy for the police is that this form of organization is marked by lack of flexibility, indifference to human needs, and a pattern of allowing **red tape** (for example, excessive rules) to impede effective problem-solving.

Quasi-military features
Most police departments are also quasi-military organizations. Police officers wear uniforms, tote guns, carry ranks (for example, patrol officer, sergeant, lieutenant, and captain), and operate under an authoritarian command structure in which orders flow one-way—from the top down. Borrowing from the military, police often refer to the "war on crime." The military model creates problems. By subscribing to the idea that they are at war against crime, police can slip

into embracing the notion that "anything goes in war." This ends justifies the means mind set can lead to police perjury, violence, and other abuses of power.

Police management styles

James Wilson, a Harvard University political scientist, identified three police management styles.

- **Watchman style** management focuses on keeping order. Officers ignore minor violations and settle disputes informally by meting out street justice.

- **Legalistic style** management places a premium on handling matters formally, "according to the book." Administrators try to reduce discretion to a minimum and emphasize uniform, impartial arrests for all crimes.

- **Service style** management stresses community service above law enforcement. Instead of arresting all suspects, officers are encouraged to make referrals to social service agencies.

Police Strategies

From the early 1800s to the 1980s, patrol and criminal investigation dominated policing. Uniformed police patrolled the streets to prevent crime, to interrupt crimes in progress, and to apprehend criminals. Whatever crimes patrol officers did not prevent, detectives attempted to solve by questioning suspects, victims, and witnesses. Research since the 1960s has shown the limits of both patrol and investigation for controlling crime. In the 1990s, the police adopted **proactive policing strategies** in which police initiate action instead of waiting for calls.

Patrol

Patrol remains the backbone of police operations. It consumes most of the resources of police agencies. On patrol, a police officer makes regular circuits or passes through a specific area called a **beat.** Officers sometimes patrol on foot but usually ride in cars. The main advantage of car patrol over foot patrol is increased efficiency of coverage. A disadvantage of car patrol is that it reduces police contacts with citizens. Studies of foot patrol indicate that these patrols are costly and do not reduce crime. They do, however, make citizens less fearful of crime and improve citizen attitudes toward the police.

Patrol has three parts: answering calls, maintaining a police presence to deter crime, and probing suspicious circumstances. Of these, the second, **preventive patrol,** is the most controversial. A presumed advantage of patrol is that police cars cruising randomly through city streets supposedly create the feeling that the police are everywhere.

The Kansas City Preventive Patrol Experiment

Does random patrol in marked police cars really deter would-be criminals from breaking the law? Does it actually make law-abiding people feel safe? Does increasing the number of police reduce crime rates? In a controlled experiment done in Kansas City, Missouri, during the 1970s, researchers divided a 15-beat area into three sections. In one area, the "reactive area," police withdrew all preventive patrol and entered only upon citizen requests for assistance. In another section, the "proactive area," police raised patrol to four times the normal level. The third section, in which the police maintained the usual level of patrol, served as a control.

The three areas were essentially alike, except that the citizens and criminals in two groups were exposed to preventive patrol, and the citizens and criminals in the other area were not exposed to preventive patrol. If the researchers had found crime rates to be significantly lower in the two areas with higher levels of patrol, they could have concluded that patrol does indeed cause crime rates to drop. Results showed that level of patrol had little effect on crime rates. Additionally, level of patrol had little influence on citizens' fear of crime or their satisfaction with the police.

Interpreting the Kansas City study

Carl Klockars, a University of Delaware professor, says, "It makes about as much sense to have police patrol routinely in cars to fight crime as it does to have firemen patrol routinely in fire trucks to fight fire." Echoing this sentiment, many police departments in the United States shifted their focus from law enforcement to maintaining the order and serving the public. James Wilson interpreted the results differently. He argues that the Kansas City study shows only that random patrol is of questionable value. He points out that other types of patrol, such as foot patrols or patrols in unmarked cars, might reduce crime. Most observers agree on one thing: Simply increasing the number of police doesn't reduce crime. There is a consensus among experts that the number of police is not as important as what the police are doing.

Proactive policing

While the mere presence of police in an area may not deter crime, aggressive patrol may make a difference. Proactive police operations focus on the concentration of crime in certain offenders, places, and victims. Proactive operations include using decoys, going undercover, raiding, relying on informants, stopping and frisking suspects, shadowing repeat offenders, policing repeat-complaint locations, and saturating an area with police to maintain order.

Because crime is not evenly distributed throughout a community, it stands to reason that some places need more patrol than others. The tradition of giving each neighborhood an equal amount of patrol wastes police resources. A smarter use of resources would concentrate patrol on high-crime times and places. The **Minneapolis 911 study,** for example, centered around hot spots. This study discovered that a small number of locations in Minneapolis accounted for a disproportionate number of the calls for police service. Brief periods of intensive patrolling reduced or displaced robberies and other offenses in high-crime areas.

In another proactive strategy, **aggressive field interrogation,** the police check out suspicious persons and places. In the **San Diego Field Interrogation Study,** officers frequently stopped and asked people what they were doing. This strategy led to large drops in robbery, burglary, theft, auto theft, assault, sex crimes, malicious mischief, and disturbances.

In **undercover police operations,** still another proactive strategy, the police use covert means to identify criminal activity while it is happening. In New York City, the Street Crimes Unit (SCU) of the New York Police Department employs undercover officers to apprehend muggers. Officers disguised as potential victims walk the streets. When a mugger attacks one of these decoys, plainclothes surveillance officers who are dressed to blend in to the area intervene and arrest the mugger.

Investigation

The TV image of detectives is that they sleuth out clues to solve most crimes. In the real world, however, police clear only 21 percent of all reported index crimes. Moreover, research suggests that detective work is boring and requires a good deal of paperwork. Finally, studies show that investigations seldom solve crimes because most crimes betray scant leads.

What do detectives do? If a crime has been committed but the police haven't identified or apprehended the suspect, detectives gather information that permits the identification and arrest of the perpetrator of the crime. On some occasions, detectives assume false identities, or "go undercover." Undercover work can be useful in getting information on future criminal activity. Four important steps a detective takes to solve a crime are interviewing victims and witnesses, surveying the crime scene, collecting physical evidence, and using informants.

Several studies raise questions about the value of investigations in apprehending offenders. The National Institute of Justice (NIJ) sponsored studies that show that no amount of investigation will solve many serious crimes. The **Rand Corporation study of investigators** found that most crimes are cleared by patrol officers making arrests at crime scenes.

Special operations

In big cities, special units deal with specific types of crime. The most common of such units are for traffic and drugs. Departmental policies guide traffic enforcement. Some departments expect officers to write a certain number of tickets each day. Similarly, some departments operate drunk-driver checkpoints and other programs to target intoxicated people who operate motor vehicles. Departmental policies also dictate drug enforcement.

Most big-city police departments have a special unit for enforcing drug laws. Officers working in these units engage in **police crackdowns.** The aim of crackdowns is to sharply increase police activity to get the largest number of drug arrests and to stop street dealing. Officers employ undercover and buy-and-bust operations (in which officers pretend to be buyers). Police also use **sweeps** (in which the police arrest all those suspected of drug-related crimes), raids on apartments and other dwellings (in which officers rely on no-knock search warrants to attack drug dealing as it moves inside from the streets), asset forfeiture, and reverse **stings** (in which officers pose as sellers instead of buyers). Police crackdowns on drugs have produced mixed results. It is unclear whether these operations shift the drug market to other areas or actually reduce the availability of drugs.

Great Debates in Criminal Justice: Does Community Policing
Prevent Crime?

A growing consensus within police circles is that **community policing** is the best strategy for fighting crime in residential neighborhoods. This strategy is based on **police-community reciprocity**—the
police and public cooperate to prevent and to solve crimes. An important premise of this approach is that police should fight crime *locally*
rather than follow dictates from Washington, D.C. Community policing often features **decentralization of command** through substations
to increase police-citizen interaction. It also involves **foot patrol** so
police can walk and talk with citizens. New York City and other metropolitan areas incorporate into community policing a zero tolerance
attitude toward minor crimes and disorder to enhance feelings of
community safety.

Community policing does prevent crime
To prove the effectiveness of community policing, proponents point to
testimonials from police chiefs and mayors from various communities.

1. Many chiefs of police and mayors credit community policing
    with lowering crime rates. They claim that community policing
    has restored order in neighborhoods where once open-air drug
    markets thrived and gangs hung out. New York City is a prime
    example. The **zero tolerance policy,** which has been given a
    showcase in New York City, holds that no crime—not the
    breaking of a window, not the jumping of a turnstile, not drink-
    ing in public—is too insignificant to capture the swift,
    decisive attention of the police.

2. Arrest more petty offenders and make more arrests for petty
    offenses today, goes the reasoning, and you will have fewer
    hard-core criminals tomorrow. Under Mayor Rudolph Giuliani,
    the NYPD returned to a policy of proactive policing, frisking
    more than 45,000 suspects for guns and other weapons in 1997

and 1998. According to police officials, New Yorkers are getting results that range from fewer panhandlers to fewer shootings and murders.

Community policing does not prevent crime

Critics of community policing attack this approach to crime-fighting from different angles.

1. No one knows what community policing is, according to criminal justice professor Carl Klockars. Even though a majority of police departments in America claim to be doing community policing, the differences between the actual operations may be significant. Community policing as it is organized in New York is different from its practice in Chicago, Washington, and Philadelphia. The lack of precision in defining community policing makes it impossible to say with any certainty that community policing is causing crime rates to decrease.

2. The evidence from particular communities used to demonstrate that community policing reduces crime is suspect. By appealing to anecdotal evidence to support the claim that community policing reduces crime, proponents make a hasty generalization on the basis of a very few and possibly unrepresentative cases.

3. The correlation between falling crime rates and the establishment of community policing may be coincidental. The fact is that over the past few years crime has been declining and has done so in communities where there is no community policing.

4. Police brutality can be an unintended outgrowth of aggressive policing. There is a thin line between law enforcement that is aptly forceful and law enforcement that is unduly brutal or abusive. The New York police stepped over the line in the 1997 sodomizing torture of Haitian immigrant Abner Louima in a Brooklyn station house and in the 1999 killing of Amadou Diallo, an unarmed African immigrant, in a fusillade of police fire in the Bronx. Underlying this problem is the recurring tension between public safety and civil liberties. If the police become more aggressive, the streets may become safer, but innocent people's rights may be compromised as a result.

Evaluating community policing

To date, no scientific evaluations of community policing are available. Until such evaluations become available, one would be jumping to conclusions to say that community policing does or doesn't work.

POLICE
FUNCTION

As far as they were concerned, Clayton Searle, a Los Angeles narcotics detective, and the federal drug agent with him were just doing their jobs on March 15, 1991, when they noticed a black man walking toward them. The pair had just arrested a suspected drug courier who they believed was there to pick up a shipment of cocaine. When the black man was about 40 feet away, he abruptly turned, set down his attaché case, and walked to a row of pay telephones. The two police officers moved in and began questioning their new suspect. A heated argument followed, which ended with the black man falling or being thrown to the floor. He finally was handcuffed and led off for questioning.

The suspect was Joe Morgan, a broadcaster for ESPN and a former Cincinnati Reds second baseman who was inducted into the National Baseball Hall of Fame. Morgan sued the agents and the city of Los Angeles for false arrest, illegal detention, battery, excessive use of force, false imprisonment, and intentional infliction of emotional distress. Morgan claimed the police had unfairly targeted him because of his race and because he fit the profile of a drug courier. A federal jury awarded Morgan $540,000 in this lawsuit. After the trial, Morgan told reporters, "I didn't do it for the money. I believe in law and order, but it has to be applied to the police as well as everyone else."

Criminal Procedure and the Constitution

The late Justice William O. Douglas would agree with Joe Morgan. "A civilized system of law is as much concerned with the means employed to bring people to justice, as it is with ends," Douglas once said, "A first principle of jurisprudence is that the ends do not justify the means."

Criminal procedure

Criminal procedure is a branch of constitutional law concerned with the rules of law governing the procedures by which authorities investigate, prosecute, and adjudicate crimes. Specific provisions of the U.S. Constitution restrict the police. In addition, state constitutions, federal and state statutes, court decisions, and administrative rules circumscribe how the police gather information and deal with criminal suspects. The framers of the U.S. Constitution sought to balance the government's interest in crime control with the privacy and liberty rights of innocent, suspected, and convicted individuals. Two provisions of the Constitution apply specifically to balancing police powers and citizens' rights—the Fourth and Fifth Amendments.

- **The Fourth Amendment:** "The right of the people to be secure in their persons, houses, papers and effects, against unreasonable searches and seizures, shall not be violated, and no Warrants shall issue, but upon probable cause, supported by Oath or affirmation, and particularly describing the place to be searched, and the persons or things to be seized."

- **The Fifth Amendment:** "No person . . . shall be compelled in any criminal case to be a witness against himself, nor be deprived of life, liberty, or property, without due process of law."

Interpretation of the Constitution

Key words and phrases, such as "probable cause," "unreasonable," and "compelled," need to be interpreted. Usually, the U.S. Supreme Court determines what the Fourth and Fifth Amendments mean. The Court decides, for example, whether the police must get prior judicial approval before undertaking a particular action or whether they can exercise discretion in choosing among alternative courses of action.

Criminal procedure as a zero-sum game

"Every time we make it easier to convict the guilty," says Harvard legal scholar Alan Dershowitz, "we also make it easier to convict the innocent." Making it easier to convict the guilty carries the costs of increasing the convictions of innocents and violating people's individual rights. In other words, there is a zero-sum relationship between crime control and due process. As we expand one, we diminish the other.

The due process revolution and the crime control counterrevolution

During the 1960s, the Warren Court, led by Chief Justice Earl Warren, interpreted the Fourth and Fifth Amendments in ways that curtailed police powers and extended citizens' rights. Fourth and Fifth Amendment case law produced by the Warren Court's due process revolution (1961–1969) shielded Americans from police abuses of powers and protected individual rights.

In the 1970s, 1980s, and 1990s, the composition of the Supreme Court changed. Liberal justices retired and Republican presidents Nixon, Reagan, and Bush named their replacements, leading to the emergence of a new conservative majority on the Court. During the 1970s, under Chief Justice Warren Burger, and then during the 1980s and 1990s, under Chief Justice William Rehnquist, the Court has been lax about enforcing the Fourth and Fifth Amendments. The national trend has been toward increasingly broad latitude for law enforcement. The justices have been inclined to let illegally obtained evidence come before a jury, for the reason that the jury needs to know the facts, however those facts were obtained. The Burger and Rehnquist Courts chipped away at rules established by the Warren Court to safeguard citizens' rights. The result has been an expansion of police powers and a contraction of citizens' rights. This crime control counterrevolution is part of a larger public policy agenda that conservative politicians have been advocating ever since the Warren Court revitalized the Fourth, Fifth, and Sixth Amendments in the 1960s.

The Right to Privacy

The word "privacy" does not appear in the U.S. Constitution, but the U.S. Supreme Court has said that several of the amendments create this right. One of these is the Fourth Amendment. It stops the police and other government agents from searching citizens or their property without facts or apparent facts that are reliable and generate a belief that incriminating evidence can be found on the citizens or the property. Justice Louis Brandeis called the right to privacy "the right to be left alone by the government." Calling this right the most valuable of all rights, Brandeis considered "every unjustifiable intrusion by the government upon the privacy of the individual" to be a violation of the Fourth Amendment.

Searches

For police action to be brought under the protection of the right to privacy, it must be considered to be a **search.** A search involves police actions designed to find, ascertain, or recover evidence of crimes, weapons, and contraband. Common targets of searches include homes, papers, effects, and persons suspected of criminal involvement. Examples of searches include looking inside a container in a car, taking blood and urine samples, and wiretapping.

Search warrants

Once an act of a police officer is determined to be a search, the next question is "Was it reasonable?" The general rule of the Fourth Amendment is that any search or seizure undertaken without a valid **search warrant** is illegal. A search warrant is a written order from a judge directing the police to search a specific place for particular persons or items to be seized. The objects sought may include drugs, stolen goods, burglars' tools, weapons, or other items kept or concealed in violation of the law.

The standard of proof for a search warrant

For searches and seizures, the Fourth Amendment requires the government to show **probable cause.** Probable cause consists of facts that would lead a reasonable police officer to believe that the places or persons to be searched will yield the contraband, fruits of a crime, persons, weapons, or other items named in the warrant. As a standard of proof, **probable cause** requires more than mere suspicion but less than legal guilt (proof beyond a reasonable doubt).

Particularity of search warrants

The Fourth Amendment requires that a search warrant describe with "particularity" the place to be searched and the things—either people or objects—to be seized.

How the police obtain and execute a search warrant

Before going to a judge to get a warrant, an officer must prepare an **affidavit,** which gives a detailed description of the place to be searched and the persons or things to be seized. Next, the officer swears under oath that the information in the affidavit is truthful. Then, the officer tries to convince a judge that the information amounts to probable cause to believe that contraband or other evidence is in a specific place.

The Gates test

In deciding whether or not to authorize a search, a judge applies the *Gates test.* The Supreme Court's ruling in ***Illinois v. Gates*** (1983) lowered the evidentiary requirements for probable cause in search warrant applications. Prior to *Gates,* the rule was that probable cause for search couldn't be based solely on hearsay (secondhand) information. In *Gates,* the Court made it easier for police to satisfy the evidentiary requirements for a search warrant. It required judges to simply make a common-sense decision, given all the circumstances set forth in an affidavit, that there is a fair probability that incriminating evidence can be found in a particular place.

After a judge issues a warrant, the police must execute it promptly because the suspect may move or destroy the evidence The Federal Rules of Criminal Procedure set a limit of ten days within which the police must carry out a search. States establish similar deadlines.

No-knock warrants

A **no-knock warrant** authorizes police to break down doors without warnings and to enter homes or public places. The Supreme Court has ruled that no-knock warrants can be used when police fear that announcing their presence could endanger their lives or give criminals time to destroy the evidence the police are seeking. Civil liberties advocates think no-knock warrants often violate the spirit of the Fourth Amendment because they are often based on unreliable sources of information. No-knock warrants are sometimes based solely on the word of **confidential informers,** who are often criminals seeking to trade what they know for reduced charges, shorter sentences, or cash. Police officials defend no-knock warrants, saying the warrants have enabled the police to mount an aggressive assault against drugs. Moreover, the police assert that a majority of their no-knock search warrants yield contraband.

Electronic eavesdropping as a search

Electronic eavesdropping is considered a search. It consists of both **telephone wiretapping** and **bugging.** (Bugs are electronic listening devices that record sounds.) Law enforcement agents sought a record number of court orders in 1997 to allow them to secretly listen in on more than two million private conversations. The telephone wiretap was the most common device used. Narcotics investigations spurred almost 75 percent of the wiretap requests in 1997. The most common location for the placement of wiretaps in 1997 was a single-family dwelling.

Conditions under which the government can use electronic eavesdropping
Title III of the federal **Omnibus Crime Control and Safe Streets Act** (1968) places wiretapping and bugging under tight controls. Under this law, police must get a search warrant before secretly intercepting conversations. Title III contains a statutory exclusionary rule. It prohibits trial courts, grand juries, regulatory agencies, and other government bodies from using evidence obtained by unauthorized interception.

Searches without warrants
An exception to the warrant requirement in Title III applies to officers who are parties to conversations: they don't need a warrant to wear a wire or tape a phone call. The Supreme Court has determined that exigent circumstances (in other words, emergencies and other situations requiring exceptional police actions) justify exceptions to the warrant rule. In reality, most police searches are conducted without warrants. The majority of warrantless searches fall into one of the following categories.

- **Consent search:** A consent search is a warrantless search made when the person in control of an area or object gives his or her consent. By consenting, a citizen forfeits all Fourth Amendment rights. Most criminal charges are handled through consent searches. A citizen must voluntarily consent, rather than being coerced or tricked into consenting. A citizen always has the right to say "no." Police are not legally obligated to inform citizens whose consent they are seeking that citizens have a right to refuse to give consent.

- **Hot-pursuit search:** A hot-pursuit search is a warrantless search following an officer's chase of a dangerous suspect into the suspect's home, the residence of a third party, a public building, or some other place.

- **Automobile search:** An automobile search is a warrantless search of a car when police have probable cause to believe the car contains evidence of a crime. The Court permits officers to search cars more freely than houses. Due to the mobility of cars, officers may give up opportunities to seize evidence if they take the time to get a warrant. The police can't, however, simply begin searching a car because they are suspicious of the driver's appearance. To satisfy the probable cause prerequisite, the police must have prior knowledge that the vehicle was involved in a crime or contains contraband. In a rare win for privacy rights, the Court ruled in Knowles v. Iowa (1998) that police can't search people and their cars after merely ticketing them for routine traffic violations. Such a search—without suspicion of other wrongdoing—is unreasonable and unconstitutional. The Court's decision in *Knowles* ran counter to its trend since the 1970s of narrowing the privacy rights afforded by the Fourth Amendment.

- **Search incident to arrest:** Once there is probable cause to make an arrest, the Court said in ***U.S. v. Robinson*** (1973), a police officer can search the person arrested and the area under the arrestee's control. It makes sense, the Court said, to authorize such a search to preserve evidence and to protect the arresting officer's safety.

- **Plain-view search:** A warrantless plain-view search, which takes place when a police officer sees evidence in plain view, is legal so long as the officer has a right to be present in the place where he or she discovers the evidence. If an officer has a warrant to search a house for guns, for example, and finds illegal drugs during the search, the officer can also seize the drugs. Under the **protective sweep doctrine,** the conservative Court expanded the scope of plain view. A protective sweep is a quick, limited, warrantless search of the entire premises. If police have reasonable suspicion that others are on the

premises when they arrest a suspect, the officers can examine the entire premises. If the police have no suspicion that there are others in a place where they make an arrest, they can still look into adjoining closets or rooms. In both situations, the police may seize contraband or evidence in plain view.

Arrests

Under the Fourth Amendment, an **arrest** is a seizure. Legally, an arrest occurs when the police take a citizen into custody for the purpose of charging that citizen with a crime. Administratively, an arrest involves booking. Law enforcement officers take the arrestees to a police station where they fingerprint, photograph, and record identifying information about the suspects.

The standard of proof for an arrest

Police make most arrests without warrants. For a warrantless arrest to be constitutional, the arresting officer must have probable cause, which means that officers must reasonably believe that a suspect is about to commit or has committed a crime. Probable cause can be based on either direct evidence (that is, first-hand information that is personally known to police officers) or hearsay. When there is no immediate need to arrest a suspect, the police may seek a court order, commonly called an **arrest warrant.** To obtain the arrest warrant, a police officer must submit to a judge an affidavit containing evidence in support of probable cause. The judge must review the affidavit and decide whether or not to issue an arrest warrant. In the majority of felony cases, though, a police officer will act without a warrant and will make that arrest as soon as he or she is convinced that there are grounds to do so.

The basic rules of arrest

Under common law, a police officer may arrest a person for a felony when the officer has probable cause to believe that a crime has been committed and that the suspect committed the crime. For a misdemeanor arrest, however, the offense must occur in the presence of an officer before the officer can make an arrest. The general rule is that a citizen complaining about another citizen's commission of a misdemeanor must seek a judicially authorized arrest warrant before a police officer can make a misdemeanor arrest. This rule has caused problems in some areas such as domestic abuse. It has prevented police from making arrests at the scene of spouse abuse where a spouse accuses her partner of committing a simple assault. To correct the problem, legislatures have revised the rules for misdemeanor arrests that relate to domestic violence and other similar crimes.

Necessity for arrest warrants

An arrest warrant is a document that a court issues ordering law enforcement officers to take a specific individual into custody. Under certain circumstances, the police must have a warrant to make an arrest. In public places, the police can arrest a felon without a warrant if they have probable cause. In homes, police must have a warrant to make a routine felony arrest. In some situations, exigencies (such as the hot pursuit of a dangerous felon) allow the police to engage in warrantless arrests in homes.

Drug arrests

Of all the felony arrests made in the United States, about 20 percent are for individuals arrested on drug charges.

Arrests and domestic violence

For many years, the police handled domestic violence cases differently from other assaults. They hesitated to make arrests in domestic abuse cases, not wanting to intervene in private matters between a

man and a woman. A federal court eventually held this gender-based policy to be in violation of the Fourteenth Amendment. In the 1970s, legislatures passed mandatory arrest laws for domestic abuse. The **Minneapolis experiment** showed that making mandatory arrests of the battering partner reduces levels of domestic violence more than mediating disputes or separating couples. The finding that arrest deters spousal abuse spurred other police departments to adopt mandatory arrest policies. Replication studies in other cities have found a deterrent effect of mandatory arrest, but only under certain conditions.

Stops

A **stop** is a Fourth Amendment seizure. The police often stop and question people without having enough facts to justify an arrest or search. Until the late 1960s, police exercised total discretion in deciding who, when, where, and how to conduct stops.

Stop and frisk

Police have a right to temporarily stop individuals whose behavior seems suspicious, to detain them briefly for questioning, and to pat them down. Stop and frisk is justified on the grounds of crime control and public safety. In **Terry v. Ohio** (1968), the Supreme Court held that when a police officer observes "unusual conduct" that leads him or her to think that criminal activity "may be afoot," the officer can search the outer clothing of the suspect to discover weapons. Such a search, the Court said, must be based on reasonable suspicion. If officers suspect that an individual may be committing, may be about to commit, or may have committed a crime, they can stop, question, and pat down the individual. Reasonable suspicion is a lower standard of evidence than probable cause. The Court reasoned that since a stop is a lesser deprivation of freedom than an arrest and stop and frisk is less intrusive than a full-body search, stops require fewer facts than probable cause. A police officer does not have to directly observe the facts upon which reasonable suspicion is based. Hearsay and/or an anonymous tip can be the basis of suspicion.

Drug stops

Drug Enforcement Administration agents and other police closely watch airports, bus stations, and interstate highways for people who may be transporting illegal drugs. Sometimes drug enforcement agents base their stops of suspected drug traffickers on tips from informants. Many times, however, the agents stop people like Joe Morgan who fit a drug courier profile, a set of factors, that taken together, identify drug runners based on their personal characteristics, mannerisms, and *modus operandi,* or general method of operation. Acting on reasonable suspicion of drug possession, police can briefly stop and question individuals to find out if they are carrying drugs.

Critics contend that profiles discriminate against racial minorities. Some studies support this claim. For example, a 1997 study found that African-American motorists stopped on the Florida Turnpike by an all-white Orange County (Orlando) sheriff's drug enforcement squad were six and a half times more likely to be searched than white drivers. Forty percent of the black motorists were searched, while only 6 percent of the whites were searched. Researchers explained these disparities in terms of the belief on the part of the police that blacks are more likely than whites to be trafficking in cocaine on Florida highways.

Are such racially biased search procedures legal? Even though the Supreme Court upheld the constitutionality of drug courier profiles in *U.S. v. Sokolow* (1989), Justice Thurgood Marshall's dissent pointed out serious flaws in profiles. Marshall disagreed with the majority's ruling that the reasonable suspicion level of proof is met simply by the police identification of a suspect as having characteristics that fit a drug courier profile. Once the police establish this level of proof, the Court declared, a *Terry stop* is permissible. Marshall demonstrated the falsity of this premise in the majority's argument by pointing out that the *Terry* rule requires evidence of ongoing criminality—such as casing a store before robbing it—to establish reasonable suspicion. As Marshall noted, most profiles do not meet such a standard.

Marshall also challenged the validity of drug courier profiles. From journalistic reports, it appears that the "hit," or success, rate of these profiles (in other words, correct predictions that a person is indeed transporting drugs) is no better than the results that could be obtained by flipping a coin (in other words, 50 percent). Even worse, some profiles include a race/ethnicity factor which makes them racially biased and violative of the equal protection clause of the Fourteenth Amendment.

The Exclusionary Rule

The **exclusionary rule** is a judge-made rule that evidence obtained by the government in violation of a defendant's constitutional rights can't be used against him or her. By filing a **motion to suppress** before the trial asking the judge to rule the evidence as inadmissible, a defendant may prevent the prosecution from using illegally obtained evidence. The exclusionary rule usually applies to suppression of physical evidence (for example, a murder weapon, stolen property, or illegal drugs) that the police seize in violation of a defendant's Fourth Amendment right not to be subjected to unreasonable search and seizure.

Weeks v. U.S. (1914)

The exclusionary rule was invented in *Weeks v. U.S. Weeks* is premised on the idea that when the police exceed their constitutional authority in conducting a search, then that search must be null and void. At the time of *Weeks,* the Bill of Rights was considered to apply only to the federal government.

Mapp v. Ohio (1961)

In *Mapp,* the liberal Warren Court extended the *Weeks* exclusionary rule to state courts. The Warren Court held that the exclusionary rule is part of a citizen's Fourth Amendment right and that the rule was needed because the states had not devised any effective remedies to the problem of arbitrary searches by police. Some police administrators and politicians denounced *Mapp* for handcuffing the police.

Erosion of *Mapp*

Lack of support for the rule among conservative U.S. Supreme Court justices who succeeded the liberal members of the Warren Court to the bench has limited the rule's impact. In a series of cases, the Court held that illegally obtained evidence could be used as the basis for grand jury questions, by the Internal Revenue Service in a civil tax proceeding, and in deportation hearings. In *U.S. v. Leon* (1984), the Court carved out the **good faith exception:** if the police make an honest mistake in conducting a search—that is, if the police act on the basis of a search warrant which a court later declares invalid— the seized evidence is still admissible.

The Fifth Amendment's Right Against Self-Incrimination

"Taking the Fifth" refers to the practice of invoking the right to remain silent rather than incriminating oneself. It protects guilty as well as innocent persons who find themselves in incriminating circumstances. This right has important implications for police interrogations, a method that police use to obtain evidence in the form of confessions from suspects.

The ban on forced confessions

If the accused did not have the right to remain silent, the police could resort to torture, pain, and threats. Such methods might cause an innocent person to confess to avoid further punishment. In fact, there have been occasions in American history when the police have wrung confessions out of suspects. One of the most brutal incidents took place in 1936 and resulted in the case of *Brown v. Mississippi.* Police accused three black men of a murder and whipped them until they confessed. A Mississippi court sentenced the men to death, but the U.S. Supreme Court reversed the verdict. Confessions obtained by physical torture *cannot* serve as the basis of a conviction in state or federal courts. The rationale behind this point of law is that forced confessions offend the dignity of human beings, undermine the integrity of government, and tend to be unreliable.

Requirements for asserting the right against self-incrimination

The right against self-incrimination applies mainly to confessions and it pertains only to incriminating communications that are both "compelled" and "testimonial." If a suspect waives his or her right to remain silent and voluntarily confesses, the government can use the confession against the suspect. The Fifth Amendment protects witnesses from giving testimonial evidence or answering questions that may incriminate them. Testimonial evidence is provided by live witnesses or through a transcript of a live witness. The Fifth does not apply to physical evidence (for example, the taking of blood samples when there is reason to believe that the suspect was driving while intoxicated).

Confessions and counsel

How is the Fifth Amendment's privilege against self-incrimination linked to the Sixth Amendment's right to counsel? In *Escobedo v. Illinois* (1964), the Supreme Court required the police to permit an accused person to have an attorney present during interrogation. Whenever police officers shift their questioning from investigatory to accusatory, defendants are entitled to counsel.

Miranda warnings

Expanding upon *Escobedo,* the Supreme Court set forth stringent interrogation procedures for criminal suspects to protect their Fifth Amendment freedom from self-incrimination. Miranda's confession to kidnapping and rape was obtained without counsel and without his having been advised of his right to silence, so it was ruled inadmissible as evidence.

This decision, ***Miranda v. Arizona*** (1966), obliged the police to advise suspects of their rights upon taking them into custody. Prior to any questioning of suspects in custody, the police must warn the suspects that they have a right to remain silent, that anything they say may be used against them, and that they have the right to counsel. The suspect may voluntarily waive these rights. If, at any time during the interrogation, the suspect indicates that he or she wishes to remain silent, the police must stop the questioning. Additionally, *Miranda* mandates that confessions obtained without complete *Miranda* warnings are inadmissible in court.

The erosion of *Miranda*

Conservatives branded *Miranda* a "technicality" that would "handcuff" the police. In the 1970s, 1980s, and 1990s, the Supreme Court narrowed *Miranda's* scope. Although the Court has not yet overruled *Miranda,* it has limited its impact. In ***Harris v. New York*** (1971), for example, the Burger Court ruled that statements made by an individual who had not been given the *Miranda* warnings could be used to challenge the credibility of his testimony at trial. In ***New York v. Quarles*** (1984), the Court created the public safety exception: officers can ask questions before giving the *Miranda* warnings if the

questions deal with an urgent situation affecting public safety. In *Nix v. Williams* (1984), the Court invented the inevitable discovery exception to *Miranda*. It allows for the introduction of illegally seized evidence if a court determines that the police would have inevitably discovered the evidence without improper police questioning of the defendant.

When a *Miranda* warning is required
Miranda applies only when the police have a suspect in custody.

When a *Miranda* warning isn't necessary
Police *don't* have to give the warnings in these situations.

- When the police have not focused on a suspect and are questioning witnesses at a crime scene.

- When a person volunteers information before the police ask a question.

- When the police stop and briefly question a person on the street.

- During a traffic stop.

Great Debates in Criminal Justice: Are Citizens' Rights a Barrier to Justice?

Historically, the U.S. Supreme Court has tried to seek a balance between the rights of the accused and police powers to apprehend criminals. Critics assert that the exclusionary rule and *Miranda* warnings undermine effective law enforcement.

**The exclusionary rule and the *Miranda* warnings
should be abolished.**

1.   The Miranda rule blocks law enforcement from obtaining confessions during police interrogations. It sets free guilty criminals so they can victimize society again.

2.   If legal "technicalities" such as the exclusionary rule and the *Miranda* rule were eliminated, there would be less crime because more criminals would be locked up and restrained from preying upon the public.

3.   There are better means of enforcing constitutional protections than *Miranda*. One replacement for *Miranda* would be to videotape or record police interrogations.

4.   *Miranda* sends the wrong symbolic message: It is more important to protect criminals' rights than to protect innocent people.

5.   There is no empirical evidence to show that the exclusionary rule deters illegal police conduct. Expanding the legal liability of police departments and setting up compensation funds for money damages would make the police respect individual rights more than the exclusionary rule does.

6.   The costs of the exclusionary rule are too high—it impedes justice by freeing thousands of criminals each year and by establishing legal grounds for appeals that inundate appellate courts.

**The exclusionary rule and the *Miranda* warnings
should not be abolished.**

1. The *Miranda* rule has not impeded the flow of confessions. Confessions are given as readily now as they were before *Miranda.*

2. If the exclusionary rule and the *Miranda* rule were abolished, innocent persons would have fewer rights. It is impossible to protect the innocent without also protecting the guilty.

3. If we eliminate *Miranda,* then police officers could ignore a suspect's request not to be interrogated. *Miranda* is necessary to protect the Fifth Amendment's prohibition against a person's being "compelled in any criminal case to be a witness against himself."

4. *Miranda* sends the right message: courts will not condone unlawful police conduct that produces confessions. This judicial integrity argument holds that a court should nullify and distance itself from a constitutional violation rather than admit the evidence and allow the government to profit from its own wrongdoing. This denial of court assistance to perpetuate a constitutional wrong is needed to maintain respect for the Constitution and for the independence of the judiciary.

5. The real value of the exclusionary rule is that it offers a vision of what constitutes good police work. A good police officer is one who looks to the Constitution for guidance in defining his or her mission.

6. The exclusionary rule is less costly than its critics assume. One study estimates that only between 0.6 and 2.35 percent of all felony arrests are lost at any stage in the arrest disposition process (including trials and appeals) because of the exclusionary rule. (The rate of lost arrests is higher in drug possession offenses, but much lower in violent crime cases.) Moreover, the costs of abandoning the exclusionary rule are too high—despite its flaws, the exclusionary rule is the best we can realistically do in enforcing Fourth Amendment rights and protecting civil liberties.

Evaluating the exclusionary rule and the *Miranda* rule

Both the exclusionary rule and the *Miranda* rule block the police from acquiring valuable evidence in some cases. But the predominating view of most academics and most law enforcement professionals is that these rules have relatively little impact on the overall ability of the police to apprehend criminals. *Miranda* doesn't eliminate police interrogations or confessions. In spite of the *Miranda* warnings, a substantial number of suspects waive their rights and continue to talk with police. Positive effects of the exclusionary rule and *Miranda* include increasing citizens' awareness of their constitutional rights and inspiring the police to follow the Constitution.

Whenever a police department arrests a crooked officer, it trumpets the case as proof that the police can police themselves. But New York City's 1998 prostitution scandal involving about 20 officers undermines that comfortable assumption. The officers were accused of cavorting with prostitutes while on duty, giving the impression that the police were trading immunity from arrest for sex. Even more troubling was the suggestion that a police administrator leaked news of the investigation to the officers under suspicion, allowing some to elude the department's snare.

The fight against police corruption that reformers started during the Progressive era continues today.

Police Perjury

Numerous academic studies and investigative commissions have documented police lying under oath in search and seizure cases.

"Dropsy"

Mapp v. Ohio—the 1961 case in which the U.S. Supreme Court ruled that illegally obtained evidence can't be used in state as well as federal trials — caused an epidemic of police perjury. Before *Mapp,* a police officer would testify that he or she had stopped a defendant for no reason, conducted a search, and found drugs. Although the search was illegal, the evidence was admissible because the Court had not yet decided *Mapp.* The police officer had no reason not to testify truthfully because it made no difference in the outcome of the case. After *Mapp,* if police told the truth about such illegal searches, the result was that the courts suppressed the evidence obtained from them. Police soon learned that if a suspect first drops narcotics on the ground and then an officer arrests him or her, the search is legal and the evidence is admissible. The "dropsy" problem has spread throughout the United States. Faced with the choice of believing either a police officer or a drug dealer, judges in courtrooms across the county tend to accept the police officer's false testimony.

The Mollen Commission

The Mollen Commission—set up to look into reports of police corruption in the New York Police Department—described the pervasive nature of police perjury in its 1994 report. It stated that the practice of police falsification in connection with arrests is so common in certain precincts that police themselves call it "testilying." According to the commission, officers tell a litany of manufactured tales. When officers unlawfully stop and search a vehicle because they believe it contains drugs or guns, they sometimes falsely claim in police reports and under oath that the car ran a red light (or committed some other traffic violation) and that they subsequently saw contraband in the car in plain view. To conceal an unlawful search of an individual who officers believe is carrying drugs or a gun, officers occasionally falsely assert that they saw a bulge in the person's pocket or saw drugs and money changing hands.

The blue wall of silence

It is extremely difficult to prove perjury cases against police because of the informal rule among police officers that forbids one police officer to testify against another. The Christopher Commission, which investigated the police beating of Rodney King in Los Angeles, found this tendency of police to back up fellow officers to be an obstacle in its investigation.

Solutions for "testilying"

William Bratton, former police commissioner of New York, announced in 1995 a program under which all New York City police officers would be trained to give accurate testimony in court. Alongside programs to teach police how to testify truthfully, there are calls for the abolition of the exclusionary rule. Police typically give perjured testimony to cover up illegal searches and seizures. The exclusionary rule gives police an incentive to lie in order to avoid letting a suspect they think is guilty go free. Civil libertarians counter with the argument that it is unwise to get rid of the exclusionary rule until the government can put in place another mechanism to assure that the police comply with the Fourth Amendment.

Police Brutality

By law, the police have the right to use **legitimate force** if necessary to make an arrest, maintain order, or keep the peace. Just how much force is appropriate under various circumstances can be debatable. When an officer uses **excessive force,** he or she violates the law. Jerome Skolnick and James Fyfe define **police brutality** as a conscious and deliberate action that a police officer undertakes toward suspects who are usually members of a powerless social group (for example, racial minorities or homosexuals).

The incidence of police brutality

Most police brutality goes unreported. In 1982, the federal government funded a "Police Services Study" in which over 12,000 randomly selected citizens were interviewed in three metropolitan areas. The study found that 13 percent of those surveyed had been victims of police brutality the previous year. Yet only 30 percent of those who acknowledged such brutality filed formal complaints.

Race and brutality

Most brutality is directed against minority groups or otherwise powerless populations. Officers who engage in brutality rationalize their
use of extralegal force; they claim they are punishing those groups that
threaten to disrupt the social order. The importance of understanding
racism in the context of police brutality cannot be underestimated.
Many police automatically regard racial minority group members as
potentially dangerous regardless of their particular activities, gestures,
or attire. This perception of racial minority citizens as "trouble" sometimes translates into racially discriminatory police behavior.

Factors related to brutality

Some police expect citizens to always defer to police authority. When
citizens challenge it instead, some officers perceive such behavior as
constituting the unofficial crime of **contempt of cop** and use physical force to elicit compliance. **Situational variables,** such as the use
of force by a suspect against a police officer, are good predictors of
police use of force.

The problem officers

A few officers are chronic offenders who are responsible for a disproportionate number of brutality complaints. Those receiving most
of the complaints are younger, less experienced, and prone to initiate
aggressive actions toward suspects.

Stopping brutality through preventive administrative control

To curb brutality, police administrators must be proactive.
Departments in some cities, for example, have adopted special training programs to reduce incidents of police brutality. Other departments have formulated rules that limit the use of force by the police.
Preventive control also requires supervising officers (for example,

conducting surveillance of officers' work) and disciplining those who violate departmental standards. A growing number of cities, for instance, are developing **early warning systems** to identify officers with high rates of citizen complaints. These incidents should be investigated, and if verified, the officers involved should be charged, disciplined, restrained, and/or counseled. Pittsburgh, for example, launched a $1.5 million computer system. It monitors every aspect of an officer's professional life—from the number of citizen complaints filed against the officer to the race of every person the officer arrests. Police unions consider the aggressive monitoring to be an invasion of officers' privacy. But liberal reformers are pushing to increase the scrutiny of officers throughout the country.

Stopping brutality through punitive administrative control
Internal affairs units receive and investigate complaints against officers. These units inquire into suspicions of corruption, complaints of brutality or other kinds of excessive force, and situations in which police officers discharge weapons. If an investigation discloses enough evidence to prove the allegations in a complaint, the unit recommends disciplinary action. Major problems in the effectiveness of internal affairs units include the unwillingness of citizens to file complaints (because they don't trust the police to police themselves) and the unwillingness of police to testify against one another.

Civilian review
Civilian review boards consist of persons who are not police officers. They review complaints against police and recommend disciplinary actions. By 1997, almost three-fourths of the largest U.S. cities had civilian review procedures. The boards try to restrain problem cops who engage in brutality, harassment, and other forms of citizen abuse. Additionally, they strive to ensure an impartial investigation of all citizen complaints. In practice, however, departments often ignore citi-

zens' recommendations. During the mid 1990s, for example, the New York Police Department failed to take action on a third to half of the police misconduct cases that had been substantiated by an independent civilian review board.

Civil lawsuits

Citizens can seek either **damages** (money) or **injunctions** (court orders requiring police and departments to start or stop doing something that violates individual rights) and can file under state or federal law. State laws provide that citizens can sue the police for wrongful death, assault, battery, false arrest, breaking and entering, and false imprisonment. In addition to state laws, Section 1983 of the Civil Rights Act of 1871 (now 42 U.S.C. 1983) allows citizens to sue public officials for violations of their civil rights. Each year courts order officials and municipalities to pay millions of dollars in damages in these suits. According to Paul Chevigny, an expert on police misconduct, civil lawsuits have little deterrent effect because officers almost never pay the damages themselves, even when the courts hold them personally liable. Chevigny points out that general city funds, not police budgets, serve as the source for paying damages.

Criminal prosecution

Prosecutors can file charges only *after* the police misconduct has taken place. The high burden of proof in criminal court (for example, a prosecutor must show criminal intent and must establish guilt "beyond a reasonable doubt") makes the likelihood of success low. Even convictions may have no impact on police policy if police executives disagree with the decision to prosecute.

When local prosecution fails, the federal government can act to control abuses. But even though federal constitutional rights limit police powers, the federal government rarely prosecutes such violations. An exception was the federal prosecution of the Los Angeles police officers who beat Rodney King. After a jury had acquitted the officers in a California court, federal prosecutors convicted the officers in federal court for depriving King of his constitutional rights.

Independent auditors

The creation of the position of **inspector general** was one of the key recommendations of the **Christopher Commission** in the aftermath of the 1991 police beating of Rodney King, a black motorist, and the rioting that ensued. The Commission—led by Warren Christopher, who became U.S. secretary of state in 1993—proposed the position as one of several changes to better monitor citizen complaints against the police and oversee the discipline system by which officers are governed.

Deadly Force

The term **deadly force** refers to the actions of a police officer who shoots and kills a suspect. Each year the police kill about 600 citizens and wound another 1,200.

Racial disparities

Most police officers shoot for reasons other than those based on race. Nevertheless, race influences *some* police shootings. Studies find that police sometimes shoot blacks in circumstances less threatening than those in which they shoot whites.

The greatest use of deadly force by the police occurs in communities with high levels of economic inequality, large minority populations, and high rates of violent crime. Moreover, police officers are most likely to shoot suspects who are armed and with whom they become involved in a violent confrontation. Minority group members are overrepresented among victims in police killings.

Controlling deadly force

Two approaches have reduced the number of persons shot and killed by the police. First, in an act of **judicial policymaking,** the U.S. Supreme Court replaced the permissive **fleeing-felon** standard for the use of deadly force with the **defense-of-life standard.** The fleeing-felon rule allowed a police officer to shoot to prevent the escape of any person accused of a felony. In *Tennessee v. Garner* (1985), the Court stipulated that police couldn't use deadly force unless it was necessary to prevent an escape and the officer had probable cause to believe that the suspect posed a significant threat of death or serious injury to the officer or others. The Court decision forced many states to change their fleeing-felon laws. Second, **administrative rulemaking** has caused police shootings to drop significantly. In the mid-1970s, police departments developed restrictive internal policies on the use of deadly force. These policies stipulated that the use of deadly force is permissible only when the life of an officer or some other person is in danger.

Police Corruption

Police corruption is the misuse of police authority for personal gain. Examples include **extortion** (for example, demanding money for not writing traffic tickets) and **bribery** (for example, accepting money in exchange for not enforcing the law).

The costs of police corruption

Police corruption carries high costs. First, a corrupt act is a crime. Second, police corruption detracts from the integrity of the police and tarnishes the public image of law enforcement. Third, corruption protects other criminal activity such as drug dealing and prostitution. Protected criminal activities are often lucrative sources of income for organized crime.

The causes of police corruption

According to the **rotten apple theory,** corruption is the work of a few, dishonest, immoral police officers. Experts dismiss this theory because it fails to explain why so many corrupt officers become concentrated in some police organizations but not others. Another explanation pinpoints U.S. society's **use of the criminal law to enforce morality.** Unenforceable laws governing moral standards promote corruption because they provide criminal organizations with a financial interest in undermining law enforcement. **Narcotic corruption,** for example, is an inevitable consequence of drug enforcement. Providers of these illegal goods and service use part of their profits to bribe the police in order to ensure the continuation of criminal enterprises.

Rooting out police corruption

When police controls break down and a scandal occurs, **special investigating commissions** can mobilize public opinion and rally public support for anticorruption and antiviolence reforms. Commissions get information from the police department, pinpoint where the internal controls of the police have failed, and recommend changes in policy. The problem with these commissions is that they usually disappear after finishing their reports. Paul Chevigny asserts that continuing independent **auditors** would be more effective than commissions. He envisions the function of such auditors as investigating a range of police problems, including corruption and brutality.

Prosecuting corrupt police officers

Since corruption involves criminal behavior, prosecution of corrupt police officers is possible. Since prosecutors depend on the police to gather evidence and develop cases, however, they often don't want to "bite the hand that feeds them."

Legislative control

Legislators could reevaluate laws that create the potential for corruption. Such a reassessment would be based on the recognition that a major portion of police corruption is an outgrowth of laws that criminalize drug use, prostitution, and gambling. Any serious attempt to fight police corruption must wrestle with the decriminalization issue. **Decriminalization** involves removing the criminal label from victimless crimes by legalizing and regulating them. Decriminalization would contribute significantly to improving the police corruption problem. It is doubtful, however, that Congress or any state legislature will seriously consider legalizing drugs or any other prohibited goods and services in the near future.

Employment Discrimination

Police perform best when they have public support. One way to assure public support is to hire persons who reflect the gender and cultural diversity of communities in the United States.

The nature of the problem

For most of U.S. history, almost all police were white men. Before the 1960s, police departments in the United States were guilty of employment discrimination with respect to racial minorities and women. Police agencies operated on the sexist premise that policing was a man's job. Until 1972, female police officers were rare. Many male police officers opposed assigning women to patrol work on the grounds that women don't have the physical size and strength to handle the job. Subsequent evaluations of female officers on patrol found their performance to be as effective as that of males. As for the experience of blacks in law enforcement, it parallels the history of black participation in almost every other form of government service. Before the 1970s, some police departments didn't hire nonwhites. Police organizations only grudgingly accepted blacks as police officers.

Following the application of civil rights legislation to local police departments, the profile of the police in the U.S. began to change. In 1972, the **Equal Employment Opportunity Act** extended the 1964 Civil Rights Act to prohibit race, gender, religious, and national origin discrimination in public employment. The U.S. Justice Department and individual citizens sued police departments. Some of these suits got rid of particular discriminatory employment practices (for example, height and upper-body strength requirements that eliminated many females). Others produced court orders mandating that police departments hire more racial minorities or women.

Even after police agencies hired racial minorities and women, they discriminated in promotions and job assignments. As recently as 1998, black FBI agents' lawyers have accused the FBI of racial discrimination in promotions. Police agencies segregated racial minorities and women within police bureaucracies. Until the Indianapolis Police Department assigned Betty Blankenship and Elizabeth Coffal to patrol in 1968, police agencies relegated policewomen to social worker roles. Male police executives assumed that women's inherently compassionate nature equipped them to perform certain police duties better than men, such as handling female and juvenile cases. Similarly, some police departments assigned all their black, Hispanic, or Asian officers to a single patrol area or beat that reflected their racial or ethnic background. Federal courts eventually ruled that this kind of racial segregation is discriminatory.

Great Debates in Criminal Justice: Should Affirmative Action Be Used to Eliminate Injustice?

Affirmative action is a policy that directly or indirectly awards jobs, promotions, and other resources to individuals on the basis of membership in a protected group in order to compensate those groups for past discrimination. Through affirmative action, police departments have taken positive steps to correct past racial and sexual discrimination. A key aspect of affirmative action plans is the commitment to ensure that the percentage of minorities or women in particular job categories within a police force approximates the percentage of those groups in the adult labor force. To hire more racial minorities and women, police organizations have recruited more aggressively, revised entrance requirements, and set quotas. For example, a police department might require that 30 percent of the members of each new class of police recruits be black until the department's total officer population reflects the racial composition of the community.

Affirmative action should be used

Generally, affirmative action is a civil rights policy premised on the concepts of group rights and equality of results. Equality of results is different from equality of opportunity insofar as the former concentrates on similar outcomes and the latter focuses on removing discrimination from the process of getting a job, a promotion, or some other socially desired good or service. The arguments for affirmative action justify a race- and gender-conscious approach to hiring in criminal justice.

1. Affirmative action demonstrates a commitment to the principle of equality.

2. Affirmative action provides thousands of jobs for racial minorities and women.

3. Affirmative action improves police-community relations.

Affirmative action should not be used

Arguments against affirmative action dwell on its costs and question the justice that supposedly goes with compensating members of a protected group for past wrongs done to other members of the same group during earlier periods of history.

1. Affirmative action is nothing more than reverse discrimination. It is wrong for a police department to give preferential treatment to members of a minority group who are not themselves victims of discrimination in order to redress past societal discrimination. Moreover, some white officers view affirmative action as a threat to their job security and their careers.

2. Affirmative action has caused police administrators to lower standards to hire racial minorities and women.

Evaluating affirmative action

Through affirmative action, many departments have increased their complement of officers from racial minority groups. A study of the fifty largest cities in the United States found that from 1983 to 1992, police departments "made uneven progress in the employment of African-American and Hispanic officers." Today, minority police officers make up about 20 percent of the officers in all local police departments, and African-Americans head one-fourth of the nation's 50 largest police departments. Females are still underrepresented. The FBI reported in 1994 that women officers had risen to almost 12 percent of the total number of officers in departments serving more than 50,000 people. An additional problem is that female officers make up only a tiny percentage of all supervisors in city and state law enforcement agencies.

There is simply no credible evidence that police departments have lowered standards to recruit qualified women and racial minority police officers.

The power of the reverse discrimination argument depends on the details of specific departments' affirmative action policies. Such policies must conform to the requirements set down in *Regents of the University of California v. Bakke* (1978). In an ambiguous ruling, the Supreme Court held that quotas were unconstitutional but that race could continue to be used as a factor in admissions and hiring decisions.

CHAPTER 9
CRIMINAL COURTS

The U.S. court system is complex. Its organization reflects the way the country is governed. Just as there are federal, state, and local governments, there are federal, state, and local courts. Governments at all levels pass laws and ordinances that prohibit certain acts, including felonies and misdemeanors. When a federal criminal law is violated, the case goes to a federal court. When a state criminal law is violated, the case is tried in a state or local court.

Each state runs its own system of courts; no two are exactly alike. In addition, the federal government operates the federal courts. A person who lives in Omaha, Nebraska, and commits a crime in that city can be prosecuted in either a Nebraska state court or the federal court, or both, depending on which laws he or she broke.

State Courts

The vast majority of criminal cases begin and end in the **state courts.** In addition to criminal matters, these courts handle the bulk of legal business concerning probate of estates, marital disputes, land dealings, and commercial contracts. The typical state court system is pyramid-shaped.

Lower courts
At the bottom, the broadest section of the pyramid, are the lower courts, which are located throughout a state and in municipal areas. The overwhelming part of the caseload of the lower courts consists of misdemeanors such as traffic violations and public intoxication cases. These courts go by various names: justice of the peace courts, traffic courts, police courts, municipal courts. Many are specialized.

For example, **juvenile courts** handle matters involving children—those who have not yet reached the majority age.

Lower courts sometimes are the sites of trials in misdemeanor cases. They can impose fines and jail sentences. In some states, lower courts handle preliminary matters in felony cases. They hold arraignments, bail hearings, and preliminary hearings. Felony cases are transferred to higher courts for motions on pleas, trials, and sentencing hearings. The quality of justice in the lower courts is uneven. Cases are processed informally and expeditiously. Municipal courts have especially large caseloads and dispense assembly-line justice in minor cases.

Courts of general jurisdiction

The next level of the pyramid is made up of courts of general jurisdiction—the trial courts of the state systems. These courts hear both civil and criminal cases. They handle cases of serious crime—not drunkenness or indecent exposure, but murder, rape, and burglary. There are fewer of these courts, but they operate more professionally and formally than do the lower courts. No one name is used for these trial courts. In some states, for example, they are called district courts; in others, circuit courts. Only a small percentage of the criminal cases that are filed ever go to a full trial in these courts; over 90 percent are settled out of court through plea bargaining.

Courts of appellate jurisdiction

If there is a trial, the loser can appeal. To **appeal** means to take a case to a higher court—an appellate court, higher up in the pyramid of courts. Suppose, for example, someone is tried for robbery and the jury finds the defendant guilty. In order to have legal grounds for an appeal, the defendant must find some error—something done wrong at the trial. The defendant might assert that the judge should have excluded certain evidence from the trial. The appellate court will consider such a question, but it will not retry the case.

In states with a small population, the loser in a trial can usually appeal directly to the state's top court, the supreme court. In middle-sized or big states, an intermediate appellate court stands between the trial courts and the supreme court. Most appeals go to the middle level. The top court in a state system has a substantial amount of discretion in deciding which cases to hear and which ones to reject. Judges choose what they consider to be important cases.

Federal Courts

Federal courts are organized similarly to state courts.

U.S. district courts

The bottom level in the federal system is occupied by the 94 federal district courts, which are the trial courts. Every state has at least one, and larger states include more than one federal district. Over 300,000 civil and criminal cases were started in federal district courts in 1997, with criminal cases accounting for over 15 percent of the total. Since 1972, criminal case filings have increased because the number of drug cases has increased. Drugs, fraud, and immigration filings accounted for more than 60 percent of all criminal defendants in federal district courts in 1997.

U.S. courts of appeals

The next step up in the federal pyramid is the level of the circuit courts of appeals. Their function is twofold: handle appeals from federal district courts and reduce the U.S. Supreme Court's workload. Circuit courts, unlike district courts, are not one-judge courts. Judges sit in three-judge panels. If the case is important enough, it will be heard *en banc,* that is, by all the judges of a circuit. Circuit courts have a review function, concentrating on statutory interpretation and correction of errors in lower federal court cases. These courts lack discretionary control of cases—their dockets depend on the number and types of cases that are appealed. Each year these courts handle more than 40,000 civil and criminal cases. Criminal case appeals have increased dramatically because of the passage of federal sentencing guidelines and anticrime laws carrying mandatory-minimum sentences. These legal reforms produce longer sentences, which give prisoners a greater incentive to appeal.

The U.S. Supreme Court

The Supreme Court sits atop the pyramidal structure of the federal courts. It hears appeals that come out of federal courts as well as state courts. The Court has only nine justices, and its workload is heavy. The justices exercise *certiorari* **power,** meaning they decide which cases to review. Justices usually select cases that will have a broad national impact. Based on their review of a case, the Court justices either affirm or reverse a lower court's decision.

The policymaking role of the Supreme Court

The Supreme Court is the most likely of all the courts to be involved in criminal justice policymaking. The Court makes policy in two ways. First, it can assert the power of judicial review. In *Marbury v. Madison* (1803), the Court struck down a law "repugnant to the Constitution" for the first time and set the precedent for judicial review of acts of Congress. Judicial review is the court's power to declare acts of Congress unconstitutional and to review acts of state legislatures.

Second, the Court also can exert power as a maker of criminal justice policy through its authority to interpret the law. An example of the Court's taking this route to make policy can be found in the Warren Court's decisions in the area of due process. Under the leadership of chief justice Earl Warren, the Court issued a series of rulings aimed at changing the procedures states followed in dealing with criminal defendants. Notable decisions guaranteed the right to counsel in state trials, limited police search and seizure practices, and required police to inform suspects of their rights.

Judicial activism versus judicial restraint

There are opposing viewpoints on whether or not appellate courts should make criminal justice policy. **Judicial activism** consists of abandoning a literal interpretation of the Constitution in pursuit of what the Supreme Court considers to be a proper course of action. Against this position is placed the ideal of **judicial restraint,** which advises judges to avoid the temptation to make public policy through their decisions.

The difference between activism and restraint is that judges engaging in the former go beyond interpreting the law and participate in making the law. To a judicial activist, constitutional rights are dynamic phenomena. The protections of the Bill of Rights, according to Chief Justice Warren, "must draw [their] meaning from evolving standards of decency that mark the progress of a maturing society." Judicial activism is not wedded to a political philosophy—it can be conservative or liberal.

Administrative Problems: Heavy Caseloads and Delay

From an administrative standpoint, the overriding problem in both federal and state courts is the high volume of cases. More than 300,000 civil and criminal cases were filed in federal district courts in 1997, with criminal filings reaching their highest levels since the repeal of the Eighteenth Amendment on prohibition in 1933. Similarly, the caseload in state courts is increasing. In 1995, state courts handled 86 million new cases, including 51 million traffic and ordinance violations, 20 million civil cases, 13 million criminal cases, and 2 million juvenile cases.

Spurred on by tougher drug laws, court caseloads have been steadily increasing. Almost two-thirds of the state courts are consistently behind on their dockets. Excessive caseloads cause delays in processing cases. When concern about speeding up case processing overpowers concern about protecting defendants' rights, justice is denied. In recent years, judicial administration has concentrated on how to reduce caseloads and how to speed up case flow.

Reducing caseloads

Court caseloads can be reduced in several ways. By removing certain types of cases from the court dockets, caseloads can be made more manageable. Diverting public drunkenness cases, traffic violations, and drug possession cases from major trial courts to special courts can shrink caseloads. **Drug courts** are a good example. In searching for alternatives for the traditional handling of drug possession cases, a county attorney in Florida invented a way to reduce the strain on Florida's trial courts while providing treatment to persons with drug-dependency problems. Janet Reno, who later served as U.S. Attorney General in the Clinton administration, established drug courts to cope with a growing number of drug cases. Following Reno's lead, many other states have created similar courts. Most drug courts use court-monitored drug treatment for first-time drug offenders instead of prison or probation. The main goals of drug courts are to

1.   Reduce drug use and **recidivism** (return-to-crime) rates.

2.   Alleviate pressure on nondrug caseloads.

Evaluations show the combination of drug treatment and urinalysis monitoring, compared with probation, reduces repeat incarcerations among offenders convicted of first-time drug possession.

The overworked lower courts can be aided by removing private civil disputes to **mediation.** Private disagreements between spouses, friends, neighbors, and associates clog the courts. Mediation programs involving divorce, consumer affairs, and landlord-tenant disputes exist throughout the United States and are intended to promote the goals of efficiency and effectiveness. Supporters claim that mediation centers not only alleviate the heavy caseloads of lower courts but also provide more lasting solutions to the underlying causes of civil disputes.

Speeding up court processing

Case backlog and trial delay are problems associated with case overloads. The seriousness of the backlog and the length of delay depend on the court. Delay jeopardizes the defendant's right to a speedy trial. Long pretrial incarcerations could pressure some defendants into pleading guilty to crimes they didn't commit. Then, too, delays erode the public's confidence in the judicial process. The public expects swift, certain justice rather than long, drawn-out processing of cases.

To enforce the Sixth Amendment right to a speedy trial, Congress enacted the **Speedy Trial Act of 1974.** It sets time standards for two stages in the federal process: 30 days are allowed from arrest to indictment, and 70 days from indictment to trial. All 50 states have speedy trial laws, which are designed to spare defendants from enduring unnecessary delays, especially if they are incarcerated prior to their trials.

One of the more promising means of increasing the efficiency of judicial administration in the courts is the use of **technology.** Dozens of automation projects are underway in courts across the United States, including new systems for jury administration. Imaging, Internet and Web technologies, satellite videoconferencing, and other cutting-edge technologies may improve routine court operations. Electronic alternatives offer promise for streamlining court administration, saving time and money, and improving the accessibility of the courts.

Judges

The responsibilities of trial court **judges** extend through the criminal court process. From arrest through sentencing, judges make critical decisions affecting those accused of crimes. Judges determine if there is probable cause to issue a search or arrest warrant, set bail, rule on pretrial motions, accept guilty pleas, referee trials, and mete out sentences. At all stages, judges safeguard the rights of the accused and protect the interests of the public. Appeals courts judges have different responsibilities, including considering legal issues raised in appeals, examining the constitutionality of statutes, and preparing opinions that explain the reasons for their decisions.

Federal judges

Most of the federal judges in the United States come from a special segment of the nation's middle and upper classes: the cultural elite. Many are private school and Ivy League graduates who come from socially prominent and politically influential families with a tradition of public service. It is not a coincidence that all of the justices on the 1998 U.S. Supreme Court received their law degrees from the most prestigious law schools in the United States—Harvard, Stanford, Yale, Northwestern, and Columbia.

Being a racial minority citizen and/or a woman is *not* an advantage for one seeking to become a federal judge. Federal judges are overwhelmingly old, white, male, and Protestant. The number of women and racial minorities on the federal bench has always been small in comparison to the representation of these groups in the general population. In the history of the Supreme Court, only two blacks and two women have served as justices.

Thurgood Marshall, who was the grandson of a slave, became the first African-American to serve on the Supreme Court. During Marshall's 24 years on the Court, he took liberal positions on a variety of criminal justice issues, including capital punishment and civil liberties. Marshall influenced fellow justices in rulings that recognized protection against double jeopardy in state courts and the right of defendants *not* to have jurors excluded on racial grounds. He helped shape the Court's decision to abolish the death penalty in 1972 but saw the Court reinstate it several years later. On the Court, Marshall said little during oral arguments and conferences, except to train his sarcasm on lawyers presenting weak arguments or on a fellow justice. During a death penalty argument in 1981, Justice Rehnquist suggested that an inmate's repeated appeals had cost the state too much money. Justice Marshall interrupted, "It would have been cheaper to shoot him right after he was arrested, wouldn't it?"

Factors that influence who sits on the federal bench
First, it has been the custom to appoint lawyers to the federal bench who have demonstrated **professional competence.** Second, **politics** matters—nine out of ten federal district court judges come from the same political party as the appointing president.

Selecting a federal judge is a multistage process. After consulting with certain senators and the attorney general's office, the president makes a nomination. Next, the Senate Judiciary Committee conducts an investigation of the nominee's fitness for the bench. If the committee's vote is favorable, it sends the nomination to the Senate, where it is either approved or rejected by a majority vote.

If the judicial vacancy is in a lower court, **senatorial courtesy** comes into play. Whenever a vacancy exists on a federal district court, the president seeks input from the senators of the president's political party who represent the state in which the vacancy exists. The president sometimes gives these senators a veto over the nomination.

Various **interest groups** lobby for or oppose nominations to the federal courts. When President Bush nominated Clarence Thomas to the Supreme Court, for example, leaders from the National Association for the Advancement of Colored People and other groups opposed Thomas because of his conservative political views. Conservative interest groups rallied to support Thomas.

Some presidents make political ideology a litmus test. In that case, unless a person shares the president's political beliefs, he or she need not apply for appointment to the federal bench. By picking Republicans with established records as political conservatives, President Ronald Reagan advanced a crime control agenda through conservative judges who have expanded police power and limited civil liberties. Today, the conservative voting record of the Court in appeals in criminal cases still bears the stamp of Reagan and his fellow Republican president, George Bush.

State judges

The demographic and socioeconomic profile of state judges is similar to that of federal judges. Both women and racial minorities are underrepresented. State judges are heavily drawn from whichever political party dominates in a particular state. The five paths to a judgeship in any one of the 50 states are as follows: partisan election, nonpartisan election, gubernatorial appointment, legislative appointment, and merit selection.

To take the politics out of the judicial selection process, reformers in the early 1900s instituted the merit method of picking judges. The first state to adopt this method was Missouri, and ever since, such approaches have been labeled the **Missouri Plan.** States with this plan use a mix of elections and appointments. The typical scheme involves several stages: a nonpartisan committee (consisting of attorneys from a state bar association and other prominent citizens) nominates candidates; the governor appoints one of these candidates to the bench; and the new judge stands for a retention election after a one- to two-year term in office. Critics of the Missouri Plan point out that the white, upper-class attorneys, who dominate the committees, nominate mostly white, upper-class judges.

The major influences on judicial decision making

Judges make decisions on motions, petitions, and judicial policy questions. On what basis and for what reasons do judges rule the way they do?

Important differences exist between trial judges and appellate judges in terms of *how* they make decisions. Whereas trial court judges often must make decisions on the spur of the moment, appeals court judges have the luxury of being able to reflect on a case and/or discuss it with their staff and colleagues.

Legal scholar Robert Carp advances the idea that all judges are subject to two kinds of influences: the **legal subculture** and the **democratic subculture.** The legal subculture consists of rules and practices that guide decision making inside the legal profession. For example, most judges are committed to following precedent. A **precedent** is a case that serves as an authoritative example for future cases presenting identical or similar questions. The doctrine of *stare decisis* ("let the decision or precedent stand") is another important rule within the American legal subculture. In addition to precedents and other legally relevant factors, extralegal factors within the democratic subculture carry weight in judicial decision making. Political values lie at the heart of this democratic subculture.

The importance of the legal subculture

Legal precedents strongly influence both trial court judges and appeals court judges. The legal subculture has *more* influence over decision making in both trial and appeals courts than the democratic subculture, according to Carp.

The relevance of the democratic subculture

Judges' political identification affects their decision making. **Political party affiliation** is a powerful predictor of the outcome of judicial decisions. Research on federal appeals court judges finds that

Democratic judges are more supportive of the rights of criminal defendants than Republican judges. A major study of the partisan voting patterns on the Supreme Court also reports a higher level of support for defendants' rights among Democratic justices than among Republican justices. State appellate courts also show some evidence of partisanship.

Public opinion, another aspect of the democratic subculture, also has an impact on judicial decision making. It has less effect on federal judges, who are appointed to office for life, than on state judges, who run for re-election. One study of California state trial courts found that judges altered their sentencing practices in marijuana cases following a referendum on whether or not there should be a reduction in the harshness of sentences for personal use of marijuana.

Political ideology can also affect judicial decision making. When judges allow politics to overpower reason, they run the risk of accepting or rejecting claims when they have no good grounds for doing so. Justice William O. Douglas, a liberal, once voiced concern in 1974 about what would happen if he resigned from the Supreme Court. "There will be no one on the Court who cares for blacks, Chicanos, defendants, and the environment," he said. Even half functioning, he said, he would be better than a conservative replacement. When a friend asked Douglas how he would decide cases if he could no longer see to read the cases, he said: "I'll listen and see how Chief Justice Burger [a conservative] votes and vote the other way."

Justice Douglas erred in his reasoning. If individuals propose that they would reject a claim or position because it comes from a source they disapprove of, they commit the fallacy of an argument *ad hominem* (literally, "to the man"), a flawed reasoning strategy in which a person attempts to disprove an argument or position by condemning its source. Douglas, if serious, seemed to propose that, in the future, he would attack Burger's credibility or politics rather than provide compelling evidence to disprove Burger's positions on criminal appeals. The proper response to claims and arguments from sources whose credibility is in doubt is to suspend judgment and focus on the question of whether their arguments support their conclusions.

Judicial misconduct and its remedies

Judicial misconduct includes activities, such as bribery, that reduce public confidence in the integrity and impartiality of the judiciary. Most states have a judicial-conduct commission that investigates charges of misconduct against state judges. A state supreme court usually decides whether or not to discipline a judge. About ten state judges are removed each year. Federal judges can be removed only if they are impeached—found guilty of treason, bribery, or other high crimes and misdemeanors in a trial convened in the U.S. Senate. In the history of the federal judiciary, seven judges have been removed through impeachment.

Judicial independence

The nation's founders made the courts an independent, coequal branch of government for two reasons. First, making the judiciary independent would enable it to reach impartial decisions in cases. Second, making the judiciary a third branch of government would allow it to check overconcentrations of power in the executive and legislative branches. Although the judicial branch is independent of the two political branches, it also depends on them. The political branches authorize appropriations, appoint judges, and decide whether to remove judges from office.

Thomas Jefferson protested in the Declaration of Independence that King George III "made Judges dependent on his will alone." Jefferson was referring to the fact that British judges did not dare rule against the Crown or Parliament because, if they did, they would be removed from the bench. For this reason, framers incorporated the principle of judicial independence into the U.S. Constitution by granting federal judges life tenure.

Judicial independence means judges need not fear punishment for using their best judgment to render decisions. An independent judge doesn't have to be afraid of losing his or her job when ruling against overzealous law enforcement or discriminatory policies. Judges who are fearful of being punished for unpopular decisions find it extremely difficult to be neutral arbiters of matters that come before them.

Great Debates in Criminal Justice: Should Judges Who Are "Soft on Crime" Be Removed from Office?

Judicial independence is threatened. During the 1990s, representatives of both political parties have subjected individual judges to attacks and threats of impeachment. Judges who make rulings in favor of defendants' rights on constitutional grounds are the most popular targets. When calling for the impeachment of such judges, politicians often resort to making accusations of activism and being soft on crime against the judges.

"Soft" judges should be removed

Arguments supporting the position that "soft" judges should be removed are as follows:

1. Judges who are soft on crime decide cases according to political values instead of the facts.

2. As part of the criminal justice system, judges should do everything within their power to punish criminals. If the public insists that judges get tough with criminals, it is the duty of judges to satisfy the public.

"Soft" judges should not be removed

Counterarguments run as follows:

1. Those wanting the removal of certain judges use "soft" and other prejudiced terms to conjure up an attitude more hostile to certain judges than the unadorned facts would elicit. This "fallacy of loaded words" violates a basic principle of public discourse: a fair argument requires a conscious effort to put forth a case in terms that are neutral.

2. Threats to impeach have a chilling effect on judges because they interfere with a court's decisional independence. Judges are guardians of justice and are supposed to act according to the law, not according to the passions of the public.

Evaluating the proposition that "soft" judges ought to be removed

Critics of the notion of eliminating "soft" judges assert that it rests more on political beliefs than on principle or sound reasoning. They point out that threats to judicial independence are greater in many state court systems than in the federal judiciary because voters elect state court judges in many states. The election process for judicial selection in many states also raises concerns about the impact of campaign financing on judicial impartiality. Even those states that use some form of merit selection make judges stand for retention elections.

There is no question that fund-raising for judicial elections creates potential conflicts of interest that reflect badly on the independence of the judiciary. Judicial candidates who can raise the most money or are personally wealthy usually win judicial elections. For communities of color, the lack of financial resources blocks their candidates from getting elected. Setting spending caps for candidates and changing from election to merit selection are possible solutions.

CRIMINAL COURTS

CHAPTER 10
DEFENDANTS' RIGHTS

Both sides in *The People of the State of California v. Orenthal James Simpson* (1995), invoked the phrase "search for the truth." Prosecutors claimed they were searching for the truth and that the defense was trying to hide the truth. Defense attorneys asserted that prosecutors were putting barriers in the path of finding the truth. Were both sides more interested in winning than in discovering the truth?

Harvard law professor Alan Dershowitz argues that the criminal courts process features multiple goals. **Seeking the truth** is an important goal—did the defendant commit the crime that he or she is accused of committing? **Protecting innocent citizens** is a second goal. Precautions are taken at various stages in the processing of criminal cases so that innocent people aren't convicted. **Ensuring fairness** is a third goal. Courts in the United States are judged not only on the accuracy of their results, but also on the fairness of their process. Both the Fifth and the Fourteenth Amendments guarantee due process, or fundamental fairness under the law, to all citizens who are accused of crimes.

What if truth were the only goal of the courts? Dershowitz argues that, if that were so, the criminal justice system would operate much differently than it does today. Police could torture suspects and their families until the suspects confessed. Police could enter citizens' homes randomly. Courts could force defendants to take the witness stand to testify against themselves. Prosecutors could try a citizen for the same crime over and over again until a jury returned a guilty verdict. Juries could be drawn from only a select segment of the community. Juries could convict on much less evidence than that which would produce proof beyond a reasonable doubt.

The adage that "it's better to let 99 guilty people go free than convict one innocent person" expresses the essence of the criminal courts process. This philosophy is reflected in a number of fundamental defendants' rights. These rights level the playing field, giving a defendant a fair chance against the government—with its vast resources—in legal battles. Many of these rights trace their origins to the Bill of Rights, which acts as a restraint on governmental abuse of power.

The Pretrial Process

While many citizens think the real action in the criminal courts happens during trials, they are wrong in that assessment. Ninety percent of criminal cases are disposed of by guilty pleas rather than trials. Most of those guilty pleas are the result of agreements between prosecutors and defense attorneys. **Plea bargaining** is a process in which a prosecutor makes a concession to a defendant (for example, reducing charges or recommending a lighter sentence) in exchange for the defendant's pleading guilty. Even cases that go to trial are sometimes decided before the trial begins. Some experts think that the O.J. Simpson case, for example, was won outside the courtroom through early forensic work by experts and through a legal strategy that forced the prosecution to present its evidence at a preliminary hearing rather than a grand jury proceeding.

The right to a lawyer

In the landmark case *Gideon v. Wainwright* (1963), the U.S. Supreme Court held that the Sixth Amendment guarantees access to qualified counsel, which is fundamental to a fair trial. Gideon was entitled to a retrial because Florida failed to provide him with an attorney. After this decision, states were required to furnish public defenders for indigent defendants in felony cases. In *Argersinger v. Hamlin* (1972), the Court extended the right to a lawyer to all cases that might result in imprisonment.

A person accused of a crime, the Court has said, "requires the guiding hand of counsel at every step." "Without it," as *New York Times* columnist Anthony Lewis says, "she may be overborne by what she does not understand."

The prosecutor's decision to charge

Following the arrest of a suspect by the police, a prosecutor decides whether or not to press charges. The **prosecutor** is the government's lawyer. If the prosecutor decides to proceed, he or she files a charging document with a lower court. A charging document accuses the arrestee of committing a crime. The most common charging documents used are the **information** and the **indictment.** Although the information and indictment differ in some respects, each of these contains a statement of the charge.

Reviewing the charge

Although the charge is filed in a lower court, the judge in such a court doesn't have the authority to hold a trial. Before transferring the case to a trial court, a judge in the lower court reviews the complaint and determines whether there are legal grounds to support the arrest under which the defendant is being held in custody. If the judge finds that the facts alleged establish probable cause, the judge sets a date for the defendant's first appearance in court.

The first court appearance

For the first appearance, the defendant is taken from jail and brought before the lower court judge. The judge informs the defendant of the charge in the complaint, explains to the defendant that he or she has certain rights, offers to appoint counsel at the expense of the government if the defendant is indigent (too poor to afford a lawyer), and sets bail.

Bail

Traditionally, bail has consisted of cash or other property that a defendant deposits with the court in order to be released from custody. The cash or property serves as a guarantee that the accused will show up for the trial. If the defendant skips bail, the cash or property is forfeited to the government. Often, a court does not require persons to post cash or property and releases those accused of crimes on their own **recognizance** (on their personal promise to appear). About 10 to 20 percent of all felony defendants don't get pretrial release because the judge finds them too dangerous to be released or because they can't make bail.

Bail discriminates against the poor. When a judge sets cash bail at a high level, it causes the pretrial confinement of many low-risk defendants who don't have the funds to either post bonds or retain a bonds agent. Another problem with bail is that it is totally discretionary. Factors considered in bail setting include the seriousness of the crime, the defendant's prior criminal record, and the strength of the government's case.

Preventive detention

Thirty states have passed **preventive detention laws** permitting judges to deny bail to suspects with prior records of violence or non-appearance for trial. Similarly, the **Bail Reform Act** (1984) gives federal judges the power to hold offenders without bail to ensure public safety. Critics charge that these laws violate citizens' rights under the U.S. Constitution because they authorize punishment of citizens in jail before a court has found them guilty. A related problem is **false positives**—erroneous predictions by judges that a defendant, if released before trial, will commit a crime. The trouble with trying to prevent crime by denying bail to suspects who are predicted to be dangerous is that it presumes an ability to predict future criminal activity. The truth is that predictions about violent criminal behavior are more likely to be wrong than right.

Grand jury review

Just because the police arrest someone and the government charges him or her with a crime doesn't mean that the accused will have to stand trial. Either a judge or a panel of citizens decides if there is enough evidence to have a trial. The federal government and half of the states provide for a panel of citizens, known as a **grand jury,** to decide if there is probable cause for believing that the accused committed the crime he or she is charged with. Grand juries are often larger than trial juries, consisting of 12 to 23 members. If a majority of the grand jurors finds there is probable cause to support the criminal charge, the grand jury approves an indictment.

The future abolition of grand juries

It is a safe bet that, sometime in the near or distant future, grand juries will be abolished because they are the antithesis of due process. Unlike trials, grand jury proceedings are private and secret, and hearsay evidence (evidence that is not first-hand) is admissible (it is inadmissible in criminal trials). The defendant has no right to be present at grand jury proceedings and no right to cross-examine witnesses. The concept of "innocent until proven guilty" doesn't apply. Only the prosecution presents evidence in these *ex parte* (one-party) proceedings, and it doesn't have to prove that the accused committed the crime.

Historically, the grand jury was created to serve as a shield to protect citizens from unfounded charges made by overzealous and/or politically motivated prosecutors. Critics charge, however, that the grand jury has become a tool for the very prosecutorial misconduct that it was intended to prevent. Procedural rules of the grand jury favor the prosecution. The exclusionary rule doesn't apply. Because the grand jury gets only the prosecution's version of the evidence, it is likely to find probable cause that the suspect committed the crime charged. Grand juries indict defendants at a rate of 99.9 percent, suggesting that they are rubber stamps for the prosecutor.

The preliminary hearing

In contrast to a grand jury hearing, a **preliminary hearing** takes place in public, with the defendant and the attorneys for both sides present. At this stage, a lower court judge reviews the prosecution's evidence to see if there is enough evidence to support the criminal charges. The standard for testing the evidence is probable cause.

Because both the prosecution and the defense are represented in a preliminary hearing, it is considered an **adversary proceeding.** The defendant has counsel who challenges the prosecution's evidence and introduces evidence on behalf of the accused. If the judge finds probable cause, the judge sends the case forward to the trial court.

Arraignment

If a case survives the screening of the preliminary hearing or the grand jury review, it goes to a trial court. At the arraignment, the judge informs the defendant of the charge and asks for a plea. The defendant pleads not guilty, guilty, or *nolo contendere* (no contest). A no-contest plea has the same effect as a guilty plea, except there is no formal admission of guilt. If the defendant pleads not guilty, the judge sets the case for trial.

Pretrial motions

Prior to the trial, both the prosecution and the defense can make motions. A **motion for discovery** is a request for the prosecution to make available to the defense evidence the prosecution plans to introduce at the trial. The prosecutor is also obligated to turn over any exculpatory evidence—that is, evidence that might establish the defendant's innocence. A **motion to suppress** is a request to bar certain evidence (for example, a forced confession) that either the prosecution or defense intends to use during the trial.

The Trial Process

The **Sixth Amendment** specifies certain citizens' rights that apply in all criminal trials.

- Speedy trial.

- Public trial.

- Trial by jury.

- Notice of the accusation.

- Confrontation of opposing witnesses.

- Compulsory process for obtaining favorable witnesses.

- Assistance of counsel.

Although the Sixth Amendment guarantees these rights only with respect to the federal government, the U.S. Supreme Court has incorporated all of them so they apply to the states as well as the federal government.

Jury trial versus bench trial

The defendant can waive this right to a **jury trial** and have a **bench trial** (in which the judge serves as the finder of facts and decides the innocence or guilt of the accused on the charges). The defendant might choose a bench trial if he or she believes a judge will be more capable of making an objective decision, especially if the charges are likely to arouse emotional reactions among jurors. But in all criminal matters in which jail is a possible penalty (which means just about everything above a trivial misdemeanor), the defendant has a right to a jury trial. A defendant might opt for a jury trial because of the pressures on judges to find the defendant guilty. Some of these pressures are political—in many states, judges must run for re-election, and any judge who appears to be "soft on criminals" can be politically ruined.

Which type of trial—jury or bench—best serves the public's interest in justice? Some people want to abolish jury trials. They contend that many trials today involve legal and technical questions that are too complex for the average citizen to grasp and that judges are better equipped to decide the outcome. The right to jury trial reflects, on the other hand, a judgment about the way in which law should be enforced and justice should be administered. A right to jury trial is granted to criminal defendants to prevent oppression by the government. "Providing an accused with the right to be tried by a jury of his peers gave him an inestimable safeguard against the corrupt or overzealous prosecutor and against the compliant, biased, or eccentric judge," the Supreme Court said in *Duncan v. Louisiana* (1968).

The jury pool

Although juries may consist of as few as six members, criminal cases usually come before 12-member juries. The court forms a jury pool by selecting names at random from lists of citizens who live within the area over which the court presides. Lists are prepared from voter registration lists, motor vehicle registration information, city telephone directories, property tax rolls, and other sources. Those included in the pool must report for jury duty on a certain date. When a case is ready for trial, each juror in the pool is assigned a number and the numbers are mixed together. A court official draws numbers to determine which members of the pool will be the first considered for a jury in a particular case.

The right to a jury that reflects a fair cross section of the community

Until the 1960s, jury pools often reflected a narrow segment of U.S. society. Courts sought the leading citizens for jury duty. Women were routinely excused, and racial minorities were excluded. The civil rights movement of the 1950s and 1960s stimulated some African-Americans to argue that all-white juries were biased against black defendants. In 1968, Congress passed a law that prevented federal

courts from excluding jurors on the basis of color, race, sex, national origin, religion, or economic status. The law required jury pools to be chosen at random, to reflect a fair cross section of the community. In 1975, the Supreme Court struck down a Louisiana law that exempted women from jury duty. This decision had the effect of extending the requirement that jurors had to be randomly selected to state courts.

Voir dire

The Sixth Amendment guarantees the accused the right to a fair trial before an impartial jury. In order to ferret out those jurors who might have a bias or prejudice in the case, the court conducts a *voir dire* examination, which involves questioning prospective jurors. In some federal courts, the judge is the only one who examines potential jurors. In state courts, the prosecutor and the defense attorney ask questions to assess the fitness of individual jurors.

Strikes and challenges

Jury selection is a negative process, with both the prosecution and defense making strikes or challenges. If an attorney for either side thinks a potential juror would be incapable of judging the accused fairly, he or she can make a challenge for cause. Whoever makes a **challenge for cause** must show that the potential juror has some bias or some other legal disability. The number of such challenges permitted to attorneys is unlimited. Through their use of the peremptory challenge, both sides seek to shape the jury. A **peremptory challenge** is the removal of a juror without giving any reason. State law gives each side a certain number of peremptory challenges. Ideally, a lawyer should use peremptory challenges to weed out biased jurors.

Eliminating peremptory challenges

Critics charge that lawyers use the peremptory challenge as a tool to stack the jury with people who have a bias in favor of their side. Since the law doesn't require attorneys to give a reason for striking candidates from the jury through the peremptory challenge, there is an opportunity for unscrupulous lawyers to exclude persons from jury duty on account of race or gender. The Supreme Court has ruled that such a practice violates the equal protection clause of the Fourteenth Amendment, but some prosecutors and defense attorneys still use race and gender as reasons for peremptory challenges. If challenged, an attorney can give another reason—almost any reason will do—for excluding a minority or female juror. To end discrimination in jury selection, Justice Thurgood Marshall once proposed an effective solution: eliminate peremptory challenges entirely.

The right to a fair trial versus the right to a free press

Before the start of a trial, a conflict can arise between the media's First Amendment right to report and the accused's Sixth Amendment right to a fair trial. The most significant source of conflict comes from the impact upon jury selection of media coverage of a case prior to trial. Pretrial publicity of a case, often adverse to the accused and inflammatory, has the potential to influence the attitudes of many people in the pool of eligible jurors. When confronted with this situation, a judge must preserve the accused's right to an impartial jury without restricting the free press. Perhaps the best solution for a judge is to question prospective jurors to screen out those with fixed opinions as to guilt or innocence.

Once the jury selection process is completed, a judge can employ other methods to ensure that media coverage of the trial won't influence the jury's verdict. Closing the trial to parties not directly involved in it is an extreme remedy. The Supreme Court has ruled that a judge must have very strong reasons for excluding the press and the public from a trial. Short of locking out the media and the public, a judge has at his or her disposal other ways of ensuring fairness. A judge can **sequester jurors** (isolate them from the world so that press coverage doesn't influence their decision making), **change the venue of the trial** (move the location of the trial to minimize the exposure of prospective jurors to pretrial publicity), and/or **issue a gag order** (tell the people involved in a case not to discuss it with reporters).

Television cameras in the courtroom

One of the most intense debates surrounds the presence of television cameras in courtrooms. Cameras are still not permitted in federal courtrooms, but they are common in state courts. For those states whose courtrooms are open to television cameras, state law usually stipulates that a trial judge can ban television coverage from the court if he or she believes the cameras would interfere with the rights of the parties involved or disrupt the proceedings.

Those favoring cameras in the courtroom assert the First Amendment's guarantee of **freedom of the press.** They contend that viewers have a right to access to the trial process and that this scrutiny will make the system more accountable to the citizens. Opponents argue that the presence of cameras infringes on a defendant's **Sixth Amendment right to a fair trial.** They claim that being on television changes the way judges, witnesses, attorneys, and jurors act, thus damaging the entire court process.

Opening statements

At the beginning of the trial, each side makes remarks to the jury. Usually, these statements set forth what each side intends to prove by evidence during the trial. The prosecution goes first and the defense follows.

The role of evidence

Testimonial evidence consists of statements by witnesses. **Real evidence** is presented in the form of exhibits, including physical objects, such as a murder weapon or a piece of bloodstained clothing. Most evidence is testimonial. Two types of testimonial evidence may be used in a trial: direct evidence and circumstantial evidence. **Direct evidence** is evidence that has been witnessed by the person giving testimony. **Circumstantial evidence** is indirect evidence—creating an inference that a fact exists. **Hearsay evidence** is not admissible except as provided for by statute or court rules. When witnesses offer evidence that they don't have direct knowledge of (and which is based on what others have said to them), this evidence is called hearsay. Hearsay is generally not permissible because it tends to be unreliable.

The prosecution's case

Once opening statements have been made, the prosecutor presents the state's evidence against the defendant. The prosecutor calls his or her first witness and conducts **direct examination.** The defense is permitted to conduct **cross-examination** of the prosecutor's witnesses to discredit their testimony. Under the Sixth Amendment, a defendant has a right to face and question those who give evidence against him or her.

The defense's case

There are important differences between the case for the prosecution and the case for the defense. The defense is *not* required to present any evidence; it can merely challenge the credibility or legality of the prosecution's case. The defense is *not* obligated to prove the defendant's innocence; it needs to show only that the prosecution failed to prove its case beyond a reasonable doubt. Finally, the defendant does *not* have to testify. But if the defendant testifies, he or she must face cross-examination. The Fifth Amendment states that the defendant has the right *not* to testify at a trial if to do so would implicate the defendant in a crime. Witnesses may also refuse to testify. For example, if a witness, while testifying, is asked a question to which the answer would reveal involvement in a crime, the witness may "take the Fifth."

The prosecutor carries the double burden of the fact that the defendant is **presumed innocent until proven guilty** and that the prosecutor must prove the defendant **guilty beyond a reasonable doubt.** Several defense strategies for creating doubt are

- Providing alternative explanations of evidence that links the defendant to the crime.
- Pointing out weaknesses in the prosecution's case.
- Presenting an alibi.
- Attacking the credibility and character of prosecution's witnesses.

Once the defense settles on a strategy, it presents its case according to the same procedures that the prosecution followed: direct examination, cross-examination, redirect examination, and re-cross-examination.

Closing arguments
Both sides present their interpretations of the facts to the jury, injecting their opinions about what happened. The prosecution makes the final argument.

Jury instructions
The judge describes to the jurors how they should apply the law to the facts, defines "reasonable doubt," explains rules of evidence, and lists the possible verdicts.

Jury deliberations
In most jurisdictions, the jury's final decision of guilty or not guilty must be unanimous. A jury that can't reach unanimity is called a **hung jury.** If the jury hangs, the judge dismisses the case and the prosecution can retry it before a new jury. If the jury finds the defendant not

guilty, the government can never prosecute the defendant again for the same charges. The Fifth Amendment protects citizens from **double jeopardy,** which means a person can't face criminal charges twice for the same crime. The purpose of this right is to protect citizens from government harassment. If the jury finds the defendant guilty, the judge sets a date for a sentencing hearing. Most defendants who go to trial are convicted.

Jury decisions in capital crimes

In capital cases (in which the death penalty is a possibility), jurors are often required to make two decisions: whether the defendant is guilty and, if so, whether he or she should be executed. Only after the jury has reached a guilty verdict does it turn to the **penalty phase.** During this phase, the jury hears evidence on both aggravating circumstances (for example, the defendant's deliberate cruelty) and mitigating circumstances (for example, the defendant's disadvantaged childhood growing up in a broken home). A jury must unanimously agree on a death sentence or the defendant automatically receives life imprisonment.

Jury nullification

Jury nullification happens when a jury disregards the law and acquits the defendant. Juries cancel the force of strict legal procedures when they think the substance of a law is unjust (for example, the fugitive slave laws) or because they disagree with the procedures used in law enforcement (for example, police lying or police planting of evidence).

The Posttrial Process

If the jury returns a verdict of guilty, the trial judge imposes a sentence and the defendant may appeal his or her conviction.

Posttrial motions

With a guilty verdict, the defense is allowed to file a motion for a new trial. If the trial judge sustains this motion, a new trial will take place.

Presentence investigation

Before sentencing, a probation officer conducts a presentence investigation. It focuses on the convicted person's present offense, criminal history, prospects for rehabilitation, education, employment record, and personal problems. The presentence report contains a recommendation as to the appropriate sentence and exerts a major influence over judges' sentencing decisions. In addition to being used in sentencing decisions, these reports are put to a variety of other uses as well. They assist probation and parole officers in planning for the supervision and rehabilitation of probationers and parolees, aid prison officials in classifying inmates and assigning them to prison programs, and provide parole board members with information upon which to base release decisions.

Victim impact statements

Most states permit victims to submit statements about the impact of a crime to a judge before sentencing. A few states allow the victims to speak personally in court. Prosecutors welcome the use of impact statements because they allow victim participation in the courts process. Many legal experts oppose the use of victim impact statements on two grounds. First, criminal trials should be conducted for the purpose of doing justice for the people at large rather than for gaining revenge for victims. Second, allowing the introduction of victim statements runs the risk that judges and/or juries will impose sentences based on perceptions of the victim's worth rather than on the seriousness of the crime.

The sentencing hearing

Typically, the sentencing hearing involves the arguments of the prosecution and defense for or against the recommended sentence in the presentence report. Defendants have few rights during sentencing proceedings, although they enjoy the Sixth Amendment right to have their attorneys assist them during the hearing. Defendants also have a right of **allocation** at a sentencing hearing—the right to make a statement to the court before a sentence is imposed.

Factors that influence sentencing decisions

In making the sentencing decision, most judges consider two key factors—the **seriousness of the crime** and any **aggravating or mitigating circumstances.** In general, the more serious the crime, the harsher the sentence.

Concurrent versus consecutive sentences

On occasion, an offender receives multiple sentences for multiple crimes. The judge can order the sentences to be served concurrently or consecutively. Sometimes judges give **concurrent sentences,** allowing defendants who have been convicted of two or more crimes to serve the sentences simultaneously. At other times, judges impose **consecutive sentences,** which means that the defendants serve the sentences one after the other.

Appeals

An appeal is a claim that one or more **errors of law or procedure** were made during the investigation, arrest, or trial. Appeals usually assert that a judge made an error in admitting evidence that was gathered in violation of the accused's rights or made errors in courtroom rulings. Appeals are based on questions of law or procedure, not on questions of the defendant's guilt or innocence. Neither the federal government nor the states can appeal an acquittal (a verdict of not guilty).

An appellate court can **affirm** (uphold) the decision of the lower court or it can **reverse** (overturn) the lower court's decision. Of those who appeal, 20 percent have their convictions overturned. If an appellate court discovers a **harmless error** (an unimportant or insignificant denial of a constitutional right), it still affirms. But if an appellate court finds a serious error that affects substantial constitutional rights, it reverses. Instead of setting the defendant free, the appellate court sends the case back to the trial court for a new trial. The prosecutor then decides whether to retry the case. If the prosecutor reinstates criminal charges, there is no double jeopardy problem because the reversal makes the first trial **moot** (for legal purposes, the first trial never happened). Often the defendant is tried for a second time, but not always. On occasion, the appellate court will allow a retrial only with key prosecutorial evidence excluded from the second trial because the appellate court deems it inadmissible.

Great Debates in Criminal Justice: Should
Plea Bargaining Be Abolished?

Plea bargaining is a controversial part of the justice process.

Plea bargaining should be abolished
Arguments for abolition of plea bargaining raise issues of rights, fairness, and just punishment.

1. Plea bargaining is unfair because defendants forfeit some of their rights, including the right to trial by jury.

2. Plea bargaining allow criminals to defeat justice, thus diminishing the public's respect for the criminal justice process.

---

3. The practice of giving criminals who plea bargain lighter sentences results in unjust sentences in which the punishment is too lenient given the severity of the crime.

4. Plea bargaining raises the possibility that innocent people will plead guilty to crimes they didn't commit.

Plea bargaining should not be abolished
Defenders of plea bargaining stress its practical benefits.

1. Plea bargaining allows criminal justice personnel to individualize punishments and make them less severe.

2. Plea bargaining is an administrative necessity—without it, courts would be flooded and the justice process would get bogged down.

3. Plea bargaining saves the prosecution, the courts, and the defendant the costs of going to trial.

Evaluating plea bargaining
Because of the practical benefits of plea bargaining, it is doubtful it will be eliminated anytime soon. At this time, the consensus is that any injustice and unfairness that plea bargaining may introduce into the justice process is at least offset by benefits flowing to both the state and the defendant.

CHAPTER 11
PROSECUTORS

In 1997, Manhattan District Attorney Robert Morgenthau declined to seek the death penalty in a high-profile case involving the murder of a New York City police officer. Morgenthau announced he would seek life without parole—as opposed to capital punishment—for Scott Schneiderman, accused in the murder of Officer Anthony Sanchez. All district attorneys enjoy discretion in the application of death-penalty statutes. In fact, they must carefully consider a range of potentially mitigating circumstances that would rule out capital punishment. Morgenthau's general opposition to capital punishment was well-known, but he had said he would consider individual death-penalty cases as they presented themselves. New York Governor Pataki called Morgenthau's decision "disappointing," adding, "In my view, the death penalty should have been sought in this case." But, as the *New York Post* editorialized, "the Manhattan D.A. is no softy when it comes to violent crime—and if anybody has earned the right to have a judgment call of this sort respected, it's Bob Morgenthau."

In making a judgment call in the Schneiderman case, Morgenthau wrestled with what is known as the **prosecutor's dilemma.** The prosecutor, as the trial lawyer for the government in criminal cases, investigates possible violations of the law, determines the criminal charges, reviews applications for arrest and search warrants, subpoenas witnesses, enters into plea bargains, tries criminal cases, and recommends sentences to courts upon convictions. But the task of the prosecutor is something more. The prosecutor is the representative of the government upon whom the courts and the rest of society impose an ethical standard that transcends the prosecutor's duty to convict guilty persons. In *Berger v. U.S.* (1935), Justice Sutherland articulated the prosecutor's **higher duty of fairness** when he declared that a prosecutor's duty is not just to win a case, but to do justice.

The prosecutor's twofold aim, in Sutherland's view, is "that guilt shall not escape or innocence suffer." According to Sutherland, a prosecutor "may strike hard blows" in trying to convict defendants, but he or she is "not at liberty to strike foul ones." It is as much a prosecutor's duty "to refrain from improper methods calculated to produce a wrongful conviction as it is to use every legitimate means to bring about a just one."

Types of Prosecutors

Prosecutors at different levels of government prosecute different types of crimes.

U.S. attorneys

At the federal level, prosecutors are known as U.S. attorneys. There is a U.S. attorney for each federal court district in the United States. The president appoints U.S. attorneys, who mainly serve as administrators. Assistant U.S. attorneys handle the bulk of the trial work. The **U.S. attorney general,** who is the chief law enforcement officer in the United States and the head of the Department of Justice, has supervisory responsibility over U.S. attorneys. The 94 U.S. attorneys and nearly 2,000 assistant federal prosecutors aggressively investigate violations of federal laws, such as white-collar crime, drug trafficking, and public corruption.

District attorneys

On the state, county, and municipal levels of government, **district attorneys** (D.A.) are responsible for bringing offenders charged with crimes to justice and enforcing the criminal laws. In practice, district attorneys, who prosecute the bulk of criminal cases in the United States, answer to no one. The state attorney general is the highest law enforcement officer in state government and often has the power to review complaints about unethical and illegal conduct on the part of district attorneys. But only rarely does a state attorney general discipline a county or city D.A. for prosecutorial misconduct.

In rural areas, the highest law enforcement official is the county attorney. County attorneys working out of small offices prosecute criminal cases themselves. In urban areas, the highest law enforcement official is the city district attorney. The typical municipal D.A.'s office features a division of labor with special departments for felonies, misdemeanors, trials, and appeals.

Independent counsels

Independent counsels investigate high government officials, delving into accusations of everything from cocaine use by senior White House aides to perjury by the president. The purpose of an independent counsel is to guarantee public confidence in the impartiality of any criminal investigation into conduct of top officials in the executive branch of the federal government.

Some independent counsels have been harshly criticized for taking too long, spending too much, or criminalizing conduct other prosecutors would most often not bother with. Under the federal government's independent counsel law, the U.S. attorney general can appoint an independent counsel when the attorney general receives from a credible source specific allegations of wrongdoing by a high-ranking government official. By 1999, the office of independent counsel had become so politicized and partisan that critics were calling for the repeal of the independent counsel law.

Prosecutorial Discretion

As an elected or appointed official, the prosecutor is the most powerful official in the criminal justice system. Prosecutors exercise unfettered discretion, deciding who to charge with a crime, what charges to file, when to drop the charges, whether or not to plea bargain, and how to allocate prosecutorial resources. In jurisdictions where the death penalty is in force, the prosecutor literally decides who should live and who should die by virtue of the charging decision.

Criminal justice professors Joseph Senna and Larry Siegel propose the true measure of a prosecutor. In their view, a litmus test for the integrity of a prosecutor is how he or she answers the following question: "When you exercise discretion, are you more concerned with fairness, the likelihood of conviction, or political considerations?"

Prosecutors exercise the most discretion in three areas of decision making: the decision to file charges, the decision to dismiss charges, and plea bargaining.

Charging

Once an arrest is made, a prosecutor screens the case to determine if it should be prosecuted or dropped. The **decision to prosecute** is based on the following factors:

- The sufficiency of the evidence linking the suspect to the offense.

- The seriousness of the offense.

- The size of the court's caseload.

- The need to conserve prosecutorial resources for more serious cases.

- The availability of alternatives to formal prosecution.

- The defendant's culpability (moral blameworthiness).

- The defendant's criminal record.

- The defendant's willingness to cooperate with the investigation or prosecution of others.

Dropping charges

After a prosecutor files a charge, the prosecutor can reduce the charge in exchange for a guilty plea or enter a ***nolle prosequi (nol. pros.).*** A *nolle prosequi* is a formal statement by a prosecutor declaring that a case is discontinued. Reasons for entering a *nol. pros.* include insufficient evidence, inadmissible evidence, false accusations, and the trivial nature of some crimes.

Plea bargaining

Prosecutors also exercise discretion in negotiating pleas with defense counsel. A **plea bargain** is an agreement in which a prosecutor permits a defendant to plead guilty in exchange for a concession, such as reducing the charges or recommending a lenient sentence. There are advantages of plea bargaining to both the accused and the state. For the accused, it offers the possibilities of a reduced sentence and cheaper legal representation. For the government, it reduces the financial costs of prosecution, improves the efficiency of the courts by having fewer cases go to full trials, and allows the prosecution to devote its resources to the more serious cases.

Important Relationships for Prosecutors

To be successful, prosecutors must have the cooperation of the police, judges, victims, and witnesses. These actors in criminal justice, in turn, depend on prosecutors.

Police

If a prosecutor doesn't have the cooperation of the police, he or she will encounter problems in investigating and in presenting evidence in court. Police depend on prosecutors almost as much as prosecutors depend on them. By sending cases back for further investigation and refusing to approve arrest warrants, prosecutors influence the police.

Police depend on prosecutors to advise them about legal issues in criminal cases and to train police officers in securing warrants, making legal arrests, and interrogating suspects. This interdependence creates a unique problem for prosecutors, who sometimes find themselves forced to either press charges against police officers for brutality or perjury—which will impair cooperation—or condone or cover up police crime—which is unethical.

Victims and witnesses

Many prosecutors prefer not to press charges if the main victim is unwilling to cooperate. Prosecutors' willingness to prosecute is sometimes based on their evaluation of a victim's role in the victimization and the victim's credibility as a witness. If the victim precipitated the crime through actions or words, the prosecutor will be less likely to press charges. If the victim has a criminal record, the prosecutor may not proceed with a case because a jury might not regard an ex-con as a credible witness. For their part, victims and witnesses also need prosecutors. Unless the prosecutor takes a case forward, the victim has no chance to receive restitution or get revenge. In certain types of cases, such as those involving organized-crime groups, witnesses need protection in order to stay alive to testify in court. The U.S. Marshals Service operates the Witness Security Program, which provides witnesses with new identities and security.

Judges and courts

Prosecutors must try to "read" judges. They need to predict what kind of sentence a judge is likely to mete out in a certain type of case and whether or not a judge will accept a plea agreement. A prosecutor might decide to drop a case rather than try it before a judge who the prosecutor knows will impose a lenient sentence or might opt not to enter into plea negotiations if the judge assigned to the case can't be counted on to support a plea bargain in court. In the case of the infamous gangster

Al Capone, U.S. Attorney George E.Q. Johnson suffered great professional embarrassment when a judge nixed a plea agreement under which Capone would plead guilty in exchange for a short prison sentence.

Management Policies

Prosecutors formulate various policies that dictate which types of crime to pursue, how much evidence is necessary to file criminal charges, and when to plea bargain.

Three models of prosecution policy

Joan Jacoby, executive director of the Jefferson Institute for Justice Studies in Washington, D.C., designed three models of how prosecutors manage their offices.

In the **legal sufficiency model,** the presence of the minimum legal elements of a crime triggers the prosecution of a case. Under this model, a prosecutor's office accepts many cases for prosecution but settles most through plea bargains.

Prosecutors using a **system efficiency model** focus on speeding up the processing of cases, reducing court backlogs, and conserving prosecutorial and court resources. To accomplish these goals, they screen out weak cases at intake and downgrade felonies to misdemeanors in order to dispose of cases through plea bargaining.

In the **trial sufficiency model,** prosecutors file charges only in cases in which there is enough evidence to ensure conviction and make only minimal use of plea bargaining. Prosecutors adhering to this model require good police work and competent trial lawyers in the prosecutor's office.

Priority prosecution

Many prosecutors establish special programs aimed at prosecuting certain kinds of crimes and injustices. Some federal prosecutors, for instance, zero in on specific crimes. During the early 1960s, U.S. Attorney General Robert F. Kennedy focused the resources of the Department of Justice on racial discrimination. Asked why he picked racial discrimination, Kennedy replied, "There are racial injustices, and they are flagrant. And I have the power and responsibility to do something about it. It's quite simple."

From 1978 through the 1990s, federal prosecutors mounted a major effort to eliminate the Mafia. Using RICO (the Racketeer Influenced and Corrupt Organizations Act), electronic surveillance, undercover government agents, and mob turncoats, U.S. attorneys initiated a stream of investigations and produced a flow of Mafia prosecutions throughout the United States. No other period in U.S. history comes close in terms of the number of investigations, prosecutions, and convictions of leaders of crime families.

Prosecutorial Misconduct

Prosecutors wield more power than any other actors in the criminal justice system. They have unreviewable power to go forward with a case or dismiss charges, to cut a deal with a defendant for a guilty plea or stand pat, and to recommend a severe sentence or plead for leniency. Unchecked power is always subject to abuse, and prosecutors sometimes engage in misconduct. Prosecutorial misconduct weakens the public's perception of the integrity of the legal system and undermines the ability of the courts to achieve justice.

Politically motivated prosecutions

Given the breadth of criminal law, prosecutors can find reason to prosecute just about anybody if they have the time, the money, and the motive. Critics of independent counsel Kenneth Starr's prosecution of President Clinton allege that Starr's primary motive for prosecution related to matters other than Clinton's alleged perjury. Anthony Lewis, a columnist for the *New York Times,* calls Starr's prosecution of Clinton "politics dressed as law." Lewis claims no other prosecutor in the United States would have gone forward with a prosecution of a citizen for false testimony about sex in a civil case. In Lewis's opinion, few citizens have led such unblemished lives as to prevent a determined prosecutor from finding some basis for an indictment or information.

Suppressing evidence favorable to the defendant

Sometimes prosecutors, in their zeal to obtain a conviction, fail to turn over factual evidence that is favorable to the defendant when the evidence is material to guilt or punishment. One of the greatest threats to rational and fair fact-finding in criminal cases comes from a prosecutor's hiding evidence that might prove a defendant's innocence. Between 1963, when the U.S. Supreme Court ruled in *Brady v. Maryland* that such a practice is a deprivation of due process, and 1999, at least 381 defendants nationally had a homicide conviction thrown out because prosecutors concealed evidence. Of the 381 defendants, 67 had been sentenced to death. The consequences of such misconduct when it is discovered can be serious. Convictions are reversed, cases are retried, appeals are brought that cost taxpayers millions of dollars, and public confidence in prosecutors is undermined.

Suborning perjury

When prosecutors knowingly allow the use of perjured testimony, a defendant's right to a fair trial is violated. The Supreme Court first established this rule in *Mooney v. Holoban* (1935), in which the Court said that the deliberate use of perjured testimony by the prosecutor and the deliberate nondisclosure of evidence that would have impeached such perjury violated the defendant's right to a fair trial. Ethically, a lawyer can't call a witness who he or she knows is going to lie. To do so is called **suborning perjury.** Critics of former Los Angeles district attorney Marcia Clark claim that she knew that police officer Mark Fuhrman (who said he had found a bloody glove behind O.J. Simpson's residence) was going to lie on the witness stand about not having used the "N" word. Clark's decision to call Fuhrman to testify may have lost the Simpson case because it opened the door for Simpson's defense team to expose Furhrman's perjury to the jury, thereby raising reasonable doubts in the jurors' minds about the credibility of the testimony of police officers in this case.

Controlling prosecutorial misconduct

Sanctions for prosecutorial misconduct include appellate reversal of convictions, finding the prosecutor in contempt of court, referring the prosecutor to a bar association grievance committee, and removing the prosecutor from office.

In the view of legal analyst Bennett Gershman, prosecutorial misconduct persists because of the unavailability or inadequacy of penalties visited upon the prosecutor personally in the event of unethical behavior. Although an appellate court can punish a prosecutor by telling him or her not to act in the same way again or by reversing a conviction, such sanctions don't hold the prosecutor personally accountable. During the course of a trial, the prosecutor is absolutely immune from any civil liability that might arise due to his or her official conduct. Moreover, appellate courts can affirm a conviction despite the presence of serious prosecutorial misconduct by merely invoking the **harmless error doctrine.** Under this doctrine, an appellate court determines that errors were of such a minor or trivial nature that they didn't harm the defendant's rights.

Great Debates in Criminal Justice: Is "Headhunting" an Effective Strategy for Fighting Organized Crime?

Beginning with U.S. Attorney George E. Q. Johnson's Prohibition-era efforts to identify and prosecute leaders of the Capone gang for any offense, federal law enforcement efforts against organized crime have been based on a **headhunting strategy.** Often the offenses are unrelated to the main illegal enterprises of a criminal gang or criminal organization. Johnson, for example, successfully prosecuted Al Capone for income tax evasion rather than for bootlegging, racketeering, gambling, or any of Capone's other illegal business operations.

"Headhunting" is an effective strategy for fighting organized crime

Supporters of headhunting use "body counts" to measure success.

1. Some criminal organizations are too well-organized and complex to allow for criminal prosecutions of their leaders for murder or other serious crimes. If the government can't successfully prosecute notorious criminals for the many serious crimes they are suspected of having committed, it is proper to subject them to prosecutions for a variety of other crimes, including tax evasion, for which they wouldn't be investigated and charged were it not for their notoriety. If an individual is in fact guilty of the crime charged, the prosecutor's motive is immaterial.

2. Prosecutions of leaders of organized crime groups disrupt criminal organizations.

3. Headhunting allows prosecutors to arrest low-level offenders on minor charges and get them to **flip**—that is, plea bargain with low-level offenders to secure their testimony against **big fish** (the top leaders).

"Headhunting" is not an effective strategy for fighting organized crime

Critics claim headhunting doesn't work for the following reasons:

1. Prosecuting the leaders of organized-crime groups doesn't disrupt the criminal groups. Groups replace incarcerated leaders with other group members and adapt to headhunting by decentralizing operations.

2. Headhunting often involves targeting the easiest cases—low-level offenders as well as highly visible and public organized-crime figures. While the arrest, prosecution, and conviction of such criminals provides good publicity for the federal law enforcement agencies, it doesn't weaken organized crime.

Evaluating "headhunting"

During the last quarter of the twentieth century, the federal government prosecuted and convicted hundreds of leaders of organized-crime families. In New York City, the leaders of each of the five Mafia crime families (Bonanno, Colombo, Gambino, Genovese, and Lucchese) were prosecuted and sent to prison. This law enforcement attack generated serious instability within the crime families. Experts attribute the government's success, in part, to headhunting as well as to powerful legal weapons and the initiatives of presidents and U.S. attorneys general.

CHAPTER 12
DEFENSE ATTORNEYS

"Do I need to argue to your honor that cruelty only breeds cruelty; that hatred only causes hatred; that if there is any way to soften this human heart, which is hard enough at its best . . . it is not through evil and hatred and cruelty? It is through charity, love and understanding." With these words, Clarence Darrow pleaded with a judge to spare the lives of two murderers in one of the most famous trials in U.S. history. Darrow used psychiatric evidence to argue that 19-year-old Nathan Leopold and 18-year-old Richard Loeb were mentally ill. His goal was to keep the youths from receiving the death sentence, which Darrow strongly opposed. Darrow took three days (August 22–25) in 1924 to scorn the idea of capital punishment. He argued that the death penalty did not deter murderers and urged the court to have mercy on his clients. Leopold and Loeb each received a sentence of life imprisonment plus 99 years.

Clarence Darrow (1857–1938) was the most famous American lawyer of the early 1900s. Clever and eloquent, he earned a worldwide reputation as a criminal defense attorney and was an advocate in the true sense of the word.

He shot to fame in 1894 when he defended the American Socialist leader Eugene Debs, president of the American Railway Union, who had been arrested on a federal charge of contempt of court arising from a strike against the Chicago Pullman Palace Car Company. Although Darrow lost the case, he won a reputation as a champion of radical causes. By the time of the Leopold and Loeb trial in 1924, Darrow had already applied his skill to saving 102 people from the death penalty.

The following year, Darrow defended the right of a biology teacher to teach Darwin's theory of evolution in public school. The so-called monkey trial attracted national attention because of the participation of two celebrities, William Jennings Bryan and Darrow. Bryan, an unsuccessful candidate for president of the United States three times, was the prosecutor. Darrow framed the case in terms of a broad tolerance of new ideas in education: "If today you can take a thing like evolution and make a crime to teach it in the public school, tomorrow you can make it a crime to teach it in the private school. . . . At the next session you may ban books and the newspapers." Darrow outdueled Bryan but lost the case. Nevertheless, Darrow's powerful advocacy of the cause of academic freedom helped to stem the tide of religious intolerance in the mid-1920s.

Lawyers in America's Adversarial Justice System

The best way to discover the truth, according to the **adversary model** of criminal justice, is by having an advocate for the prosecution and the defense. Each advocate has the responsibility for presenting the facts from a partisan point of view. This system is supposed to maximize the chances that all the relevant facts and arguments will be placed before a fact-finder.

An important difference between the prosecution and the defense is that the prosecutor plays the double role of government lawyer and government representative, whereas the defense attorney acts primarily as the protector of the defendant's interests. These role differences produce divergent ethical responsibilities. As a matter of fundamental fairness, a prosecutor is obligated to turn over factual evidence that is favorable to the defendant when the evidence is material to guilt or punishment. The role of the defense attorney requires, however, that the attorney withhold truthful and relevant information from the court in a specific case—even though such a practice frustrates the search for the truth.

The attorney-client privilege in a criminal case

The general rule is that lawyer-client communications are **privileged,** or confidential. Lawyers can't reveal a client's oral or written statements to anyone. If this sacred trust of confidentiality were not inviolable, a client wouldn't feel free to disclose to his or her attorney everything the attorney needs to know to represent the client's interests. If this privilege were abolished, great injury would be done to the adversary system of fact-finding because clients would be afraid to confide in their attorneys.

Defense counsel justification for representing a guilty defendant

Defense lawyers are ethically bound to represent all clients — even those they know are guilty. Justice in the United States requires a vigorous defense to protect the innocent and to ensure that judges and citizens, not the police, determine whether the defendant is guilty of a crime. Some defense attorneys never ask their clients if they are guilty. They prefer to use the facts to focus on the government's failure to prove its case beyond a reasonable doubt and to leave to the judge or jury the question of guilt. The distinction between **actual guilt** and **legal guilt** is relevant here. There is a difference between what the defendant did and what the prosecution can prove. Regardless of what the defendant has done, the burden of proof is on the prosecution. Until the prosecution puts on enough evidence to convince a judge or jury that the defendant is guilty beyond a reasonable doubt, the defendant is not legally guilty.

Functions of the defense lawyer

The essence of the role of defense lawyer is speaking and acting on behalf of defendants. The defense attorney is central to the fair operation of the criminal justice process. The defendant needs assistance of counsel at every stage of the criminal courts process. While representing defendants, defense attorneys perform the following functions:

- Represent the accused after arrest to give advice during police questioning and make sure constitutional rights are not violated during pretrial procedures.

- Investigate details of the offense on behalf of the accused.

- Discuss the case with the prosecutor to determine the strength of the prosecution's case.

- Represent the accused at bail hearings and hearings on pretrial motions.

- Negotiate deals with prosecutors, usually involving reduced charges and lighter sentences.

- Devise a defense strategy.

- Represent the accused at trial.

- Design sentencing proposals that serve as alternatives to those recommended by prosecutors and/or probation officers.

- Present an appeal.

Types of Defense

There are three ways for defendants to defend themselves in a criminal court:

1. By using legal services for the poor.

2. By using retained counsel.

3. By self-representation.

Legal services for the poor

Most defendants can't afford to hire their own private defense attorney. When defendants are legally indigent, the court is required to provide them with legal representation at government expense if jail or prison time is a possible sentence. In *Gideon v. Wainwright* (1963), the U.S. Supreme Court ruled that an indigent defendant charged in a state court with a felony has the right to counsel under the due process clause of the Fourteenth Amendment. In 1972 the Court ruled in *Argersinger v. Hamlin* that a defendant has the right to counsel at trial whenever he or she may be imprisoned for any offense, whether it is a felony or a misdemeanor. But indigent defendants are not always entitled to free legal representation. For example, those charged with minor traffic offenses are not entitled to free legal services.

How does one qualify for free legal services? Ordinarily, a defendant who wants legal counsel appointed at government expense must ask a judge to appoint an attorney and provide the court with information about his or her income and resources. Each state makes its own rules with respect to who is indigent.

More than 80 percent of the people in the U.S. who are accused of a felony use a publicly appointed defense attorney. The federal government and many states set up **public defender offices.** Typically, the chief public defender is an elected or appointed official who supervises assistant public defenders. Public defenders represent indigent defendants in criminal cases. In states that don't have public defenders, most of the criminal cases are handled through an **assigned counsel system.** In such a system, the court appoints a private attorney to represent indigent defendants. A judge selects the attorney from a list established by the court, and the attorney's fee is paid by the government with jurisdiction over a case. The **contract system** is used in a few counties, mainly in the western states. In this system, a law firm or lawyer is paid a set amount of money to handle indigents' defense cases for a specified period.

Free legal defense services are generally underfunded because court-appointed legal representation is politically unpopular. High caseloads for court-appointed attorneys force them to pressure defendants to accept plea bargains. Public defenders in large offices in urban areas, for example, are likely to have close to two hundred felony cases per year. Another problem is that some court-appointed attorneys are unlikely to take issue with judges' decisions because they depend on judges for future appointments in cases involving indigents.

Retained counsel

Private criminal defense lawyers practice on their own or in small partnerships. Typical private defense lawyers have several years of experience working for the government, some as prosecutors or public defenders, before going into private legal practice.

Private defense attorneys set their **fees** according to the complexity of the case and the attorney's experience. If an attorney is experienced in criminal defense work and the defendant is facing felony charges, the fee will be higher than if the attorney is inexperienced and the defendant is facing misdemeanor charges. The median legal fee charged by lawyers in criminal cases was $1,500 in 1996. If this figure seems low, it's because many cases require only one consultation and one court appearance by a lawyer. For cases that go to trial, defendants pay much more.

The defense bar is stratified, with a small cadre of highly publicized and highly skilled lawyers (for example, Johnnie Cochran, Roy Black, Alan Dershowitz, and F. Lee Bailey) handling only a few cases each year. These nationally known attorneys charge large fees and build their reputations representing famous clients. For most felony defendants who can afford to retain their own counsel, the private bar makes available a much larger group of attorneys in full-time practice. These lawyers handle a large volume of criminal cases, negotiating pleas and trying to persuade their clients that they have made a good deal with the prosecution.

Self-representation

An important qualification to *Gideon* was made in ***Faretta v. California*** (1975), a case in which the Supreme Court established self-representation in a criminal case as a right. A defendant who wants to represent himself or herself must knowingly and voluntarily waive the right to counsel and must demonstrate minimum qualifications to conduct his or her own trial. Few defendants are capable of effectively representing themselves.

Defense Strategies

Defenses are arguments with supporting evidence that a defense attorney puts forth to secure the freedom of his or her client. A defense grows out of a defendant's version of the events in the alleged crime. It is intended to bring about the most favorable outcome for the defendant (for example, a verdict of not guilty or an acceptable plea agreement).

Some considerations

When developing a defense strategy, the defense attorney considers the credibility of defense and prosecution witnesses, community attitudes toward the crime and the defendant, and the nature of the prosecution's evidence. An important ethical rule is that a defense attorney can't knowingly encourage or help a defendant lie under oath (in other words, commit perjury) and consequently is forbidden to call a witness who he or she knows will lie on the witness stand. Even if a defense attorney knows his or her client is guilty, the attorney can cross-examine prosecution witnesses and poke holes in the prosecution's case. This procedure is permissible because it is the defense attorney's responsibility to make the prosecution prove its case.

The most common defense

The most common defense is that the prosecution failed to prove the defendant guilty beyond a reasonable doubt. By raising questions about the credibility of the prosecution's witnesses, the defense counsel seeks to create reasonable doubt in the minds of the jurors so they will acquit the defendant. To cast doubt on the truthfulness and reliability of prosecution witnesses, a defense attorney can use any or all of these tactics:

- Demonstrate **bias** on the part of prosecution witnesses, who, therefore, may be lying.

- Expose **police mistakes** in gathering, maintaining, and testing physical evidence.

- Suggest that the prosecution has **bribed** a witness by granting immunity from prosecution for pending criminal charges in exchange for the witness's testimony against the defendant.

- Challenge the **believability** of a witness's story on the grounds of logic or common sense.

Mounting effective challenges to various aspects of the prosecution's case costs money. Money buys resources—investigators, forensic scientists, and legal experts—that can influence the outcome in a trial. O. J. Simpson's expenditures of $6 million on his defense, for example, may have bought him an acquittal.

Ineffective Assistance of Counsel

In *Strickland v. Washington* (1984), the U.S. Supreme Court declared that the Sixth Amendment guarantee of assistance of counsel means **effective assistance.** To prevail on an appeal based on the claim of ineffective assistance of counsel, the appellant (the person who appeals) must prove that his or her attorney's performance was deficient, that the attorney's substandard performance prejudiced the case, and that it was likely that, but for the attorney's errors, the result would have been different. *Strickland* puts the burden of proof on the appellant to prove that his or her lawyer's assistance was ineffective. In a powerful dissent, Justice Thurgood Marshall (who was no slouch as an appellate lawyer, winning 29 of 32 cases that he argued before the Supreme Court) claimed that the majority's standard of "reasonably effective assistance" is too ambiguous. He asserted that it is very difficult, if not impossible, to determine whether the outcome of a case would have been different if the defense lawyer had been competent.

Several problems result from ineffective assistance of counsel. First, ineffective assistance produces unjust convictions and wrongful executions. Second, it creates an imbalance in the adversary process, which heightens the chances of governmental abuses of power and undermines fundamental constitutional rights. Third, it thwarts achievement of the goal of equal justice. Due to the gross underfunding of legal services for the poor, the failure to provide effective assistance draws a line between rich and poor. Since a disproportionately large number of persons who avail themselves of legal services for the poor are racial minorities, the impact of ineffective assistance of counsel falls heavily upon African-Americans and other racial/ethnic minorities.

The cause and the solution
The main cause of the problem of ineffective assistance of counsel is lack of resources. Legal services for the poor are severely underfunded. Even when private counsel is involved, a huge funding gap usually remains between prosecution and defense. Substantially more government dollars are spent on the prosecution than on the defense. Moreover, prosecutors enjoy the additional resources of having their investigatory work done by law enforcement. A recent study concluded that money can have a big impact on jury verdicts because money buys investigative resources, which make a difference in jury trials.

Allan Dershowitz thinks providing more legal resources to indigent defendants would make the playing field level. He recommends that "all indigent defendants . . . who have a large team of prosecutors, police, and experts arrayed against them" be given "a reasonably comparable defense team." Increasing the resources of indigent defendants, in his view, would strengthen the adversary process, making it more likely to produce both truth and equal justice.

Great Debates in Criminal Justice: Do Most Defense Attorneys Distort the Truth?

Do defense lawyers say or do anything to get their clients off?

Most defense attorneys do distort the truth
Critics of the defense bar charge that when a defendant is guilty, lawyers do everything in their power to prevent the truth from coming out.

1. The adversary system of justice encourages defense attorneys to distort the truth by making victory, not truth, the ultimate goal in a criminal lawsuit. This fosters a win-at-all-costs mentality on the part of defense attorneys, which, in turn, leads lawyers to pervert the truth.

2. Defense attorneys engage in unethical practices that twist the truth. They cross-examine for the purpose of discrediting the reliability or credibility of adverse witnesses who they know are telling the truth, and they put witnesses on the stand knowing the witnesses will commit perjury.

Most defense attorneys do not distort the truth

The main job of lawyers is to defend their clients under the mandate of the Sixth Amendment. This defense ensures that the rights of innocent people are protected and that the government is put to the test of proving legal guilt beyond a reasonable doubt.

1. The adversary system encourages a zealous and independent defense, which is necessary to keep the rest of the criminal justice system honest. A good defense lawyer can expose sloppy police lab work, racist police officers, and prosecutorial misconduct. By monitoring and scrutinizing the procedures used against the accused in a criminal case, the defense attorney makes the system more credible and more deserving of respect.

2. Most defense attorneys don't lie. The public is protected from such deviant behavior by rules of professional conduct that "prevent counsel from making dilatory motions, adducing inadmissible or perjured evidence, or advancing frivolous or improper arguments. . . ." Bar associations enforce these rules and discipline violators.

Evaluating the proposition that most defense attorneys distort the truth

While it is true that defense lawyers occasionally distort the truth, it is also true that prosecutors are equally guilty of sometimes misrepresenting the truth to win a case. Most defense and prosecutorial misconduct is an unfortunate byproduct of the adversarial process. This adversarial process is the linchpin of the criminal justice system in the United States. Such a process operates on the assumption that the truth will prevail from the conflict between the prosecution and the defense. With the adversary process, the defendant is entitled to an array of constitutional rights, the most important of which, from an adversarial standpoint, is the right to counsel, because it is through the right to counsel that the defendant is best able to assert other important rights. These other rights include the right to confront the witnesses against him or her, the right to present a defense, the right to compulsory process in order to obtain witnesses and evidence, the right to remain silent, and the general right to fairness in the prosecution of his or her case.

CHAPTER 13
SENTENCING

"From this day forward, I shall not tinker with the machinery of death," declared Justice Harry Blackmun. After agonizing over the question of the constitutionality of capital punishment for nearly a quarter of a century, Blackmun stated in 1994 that he felt "morally and intellectually obligated simply to concede that the death penalty experiment has failed."

President Richard Nixon appointed Blackmun to the U.S. Supreme Court in 1970, a decision many believed was motivated by Nixon's desire to make the Court more conservative. During Blackmun's early years on the Court, he often voted with conservative Chief Justice Warren Burger. He later moved away from the conservative block and joined liberal Justices Thurgood Marshall and William Joseph Brennan, Jr., in dissent. Blackmun established himself as a passionate supporter of civil liberties. He is best known for his majority opinion in *Roe v. Wade* (1973), upholding the constitutional right of a woman to decide whether to have an abortion. Considering that Blackmun had been an architect of the modern-day death penalty and had started his tenure on the Court as a conservative, his repudiation of capital punishment is extraordinary.

Theories of Punishment

Changes in U.S. politics have caused shifts in the theoretical purposes of sentencing. During the heyday of liberalism in the 1960s and 1970s, the judicial and executive branches (for example, parole boards) wielded power in sentencing. Legislators designed sentencing laws with rehabilitation in mind. More recently, during the politically conservative 1980s and 1990s, legislators seized power over sentencing, and a combination of theories—deterrence, retribution, and incapacitation—have influenced sentencing laws.

Deterrence

Can fear discourage crime? There has been much debate over whether deterrence works. Proponents assert that punishment deters if it is administered with celerity (swiftness), certainty, and severity. A distinction needs to be drawn between general versus specific deterrence. **General deterrence** uses the person sentenced for a crime as an example to induce the public to refrain from criminal conduct, while **specific deterrence** punishes an offender to dissuade that offender from committing crimes in the future. Critics point to the high **recidivism** (relapse into crime) rates of persons sentenced to prison as evidence of the lack of effectiveness of specific deterrence. Critics also note that there are limits to the impact of general deterrence. Some crimes, such as crimes of passion and crimes committed while under the influence of drugs, can't be deterred because their perpetrators don't rationally weigh the benefits versus the costs (which include punishment) before breaking the law. Finally, research evidence suggests that the deterrent effect of punishment is weak.

Incapacitation

A popular reason for punishment is that it gets criminals off the streets and protects the public. The idea is to remove an offender from society, making it physically impossible (or at least very difficult) for him or her to commit further crimes against the public while serving a sentence. Incapacitation works as long as the offenders remain locked up. There is no question that incapacitation reduces crime rates by some unknown degree. The problem is that it is very expensive. Incapacitation carries high costs not only in terms of building and operating prisons, but also in terms of disrupting families when family members are locked up.

Rehabilitation

"Let the punishment fit the criminal" expresses the rehabilitative ethic. **Rehabilitation** calls for changing the individual lawbreaker through correctional interventions, such as drug-treatment programs.

But evaluations of correctional treatment show it doesn't consistently prevent or reduce crime. Why has rehabilitation failed? Funding has been inadequate, so the full effectiveness of rehabilitation hasn't been tested. Furthermore, certain criminals—such as perpetrators of nonviolent crimes and first-time offenders—are more likely to be successfully rehabilitated than repeat offenders and violent criminals.

Common ground

Deterrence, incapacitation, and rehabilitation are all arguments that look to the consequences of punishment. They are all forward-looking theories of punishment. That is, they look to the future in deciding what to do in the present. The shared goal of all three is crime prevention.

Retribution

"Let the punishment fit the crime" captures the essence of retribution. Proponents advocate **just deserts,** which defines justice in terms of fairness and proportionality. Retributivists aim to dispense punishment according to an offender's moral blameworthiness (as measured by the severity of crimes of which the offender was convicted). Ideally, the harshness of punishments should be proportionate to the seriousness of crimes. In reality, it is difficult to match punishments and crimes, since there is no way to objectively calibrate the moral depravity of particular crimes and/or the painfulness of specific punishments. Retribution is a backward-looking theory of punishment. It looks to the past to determine what to do in the present.

Types of Sentences

Sentences are punishments for convicted defendants. Prescribed punishments for crimes can be found in state and federal statutes. The Eighth Amendment places limits on the severity of punishments.

The death penalty

Thirty-eight states and the federal government impose capital punishment. It is usually reserved for those who commit first-degree murder under aggravating circumstances. Defendants convicted of capital offenses have a right to bring mitigating circumstances to the attention of the sentencing authority in order to ensure that only those individuals who deserve to die for their crimes receive the death penalty. Similarly, defendants also have a right to be free from the arbitrary and capricious imposition of death as a penalty.

To prevent the arbitrary application of the death penalty, death-penalty statutes contain many safeguards. Particularly significant are requirements that limit the discretion of the sentencing jury or judge, that require the presence of aggravating circumstances, that allow the introduction of evidence showing mitigating circumstances, that mandate a two-part proceeding (one for the determination of innocence or guilt and the other for deciding the sentence), and that provide for the automatic review by an appellate court of all death sentences.

Incarceration

Jails are short-term lock-up centers normally run by counties and operated by county sheriffs. Inmates housed in jails include unconvicted defendants awaiting trial who are unable to make bail, convicted misdemeanants, and felons serving jail time as a result of probation violations. **Prisons** are long-term penal facilities operated by state and federal governments. Most prison inmates are convicted felons serving sentences of more than one year.

Probation

Probation, the most frequently used criminal sanction, is a sentence that an offender serves in the community in lieu of incarceration. Probationers are required to adhere to conditions of probation, such as obeying all laws, paying fines or restitution, reporting to a probation officer, abstaining from drug usage, refraining from travel out of the area where the offender lives, and avoiding certain people (for example, other criminals or victims) and places. If a probationer violates any condition of probation or commits a new crime, the judge can revoke (take away) probation and incarcerate the offender. Probation officers monitor offenders and hook them up with various services in the community. Probation officers handle such large caseloads (on average, 118 per officer in 1994) that they are left with limited time to track or supervise offenders.

Probation is the preferred sentence when the crime is nonviolent, the offender isn't dangerous, the convicted criminal isn't a repeat offender, and/or the criminal is willing to make restitution. Due to prison overcrowding, judges have been forced to place more felons on probation. A Rand Corporation study found that 60 percent of the felons on probation were rearrested for a new crime.

Intensive supervision probation (ISP)

Intensive supervision probation is used for offenders needing more supervision. It allows offenders to live in the community but under severe restrictions. ISP offenders can be required to meet with their probation officers as often as five times a week, to submit to random drug urinalysis tests, to work, to attend drug treatment, and to be under tight surveillance. In 1994, the average ISP caseload was 29 cases for each probation officer. At least one jurisdiction in each state has implemented ISP, primarily for those convicted of crimes against property.

How cost-effective is ISP? A study of 14 jurisdictions across the country, sponsored by the U.S. Department of Justice and conducted by the Rand Corporation, indicated ISP didn't reduce the cost of correctional services, in part, because the offenders targeted for participation wouldn't have done much prison time. The study also showed that ISP didn't reduce recidivism. Recidivism among ISP participants, however, was often related to violations of the conditions of intensive probation rather than to new crimes.

Boot camps

Offenders sentenced to boot camps live in military-style barracks and undergo rigorous physical and behavioral training for three to six months. Boot camps are generally reserved for first-time offenders in their late teens or early twenties. These highly regimented programs are designed to instill discipline and hold youths accountable for their actions. Offenders who successfully complete the program are resentenced to probation, avoiding confinement in prison. Research has failed to confirm that boot camps lower recidivism rates.

House arrest and electronic monitoring

An offender sentenced to house arrest must spend all or most of the day at home. Compliance is enforced in some states by requiring the offender to wear a small transmitter on the wrist or ankle, which sends electronic signals to monitoring units. House arrest can stand alone as a sanction or be used with electronic monitoring. It can also be coupled with fines, community service, and other sanctions. Some electronic monitoring devices can analyze an offender's breath to see if the offender has drunk any alcohol in violation of conditions of the house-arrest sentence.

Fines

Fines are common for first-time offenders convicted of crimes such as shoplifting, minor drug possession, and traffic violations. In more serious cases, judges combine fines with incarceration or other punishments. If fines aren't paid, offenders go to jail. Fines discriminate against the poor. **Day fines** are a creative response to this problem.

They require offenders to pay a percentage of their weekly or monthly earnings, thus attempting to equalize the financial impact of the sentence on the offender.

Restitution

Restitution requires an offender to pay money to a victim, whereas a **fine** requires an offender to pay money to the government. The idea behind restitution is to make the offender pay the victim back for economic losses caused by the crime. The offender may, for example, be required to pay the victim's medical bills or pay a sum of money equal to the value of property stolen. The biggest problem with restitution is collecting the money. To enforce restitution orders, a judge can attach, or garnish, an offender's assets or wages. Another way to enforce restitution is possible in cases in which restitution is a condition of probation. If the offender fails to pay restitution, a judge can revoke the probation and incarcerate the offender.

Community service

Paying the community back for harm done, through doing work that benefits the public, is the essence of community service. Offenders can be required, for example, to pick up trash in parks, plant trees, and wash away graffiti.

"Scarlet-letter" punishments

Punishing by shaming provides a cheap and morally satisfying alternative to punishment. Courts have ordered people convicted of assault or child molestation to put signs in their yards, announcing their crimes. Still other judges have ordered chronic drunk drivers to put bright orange bumper stickers on their cars, announcing their problem and urging other drivers to report erratic driving to the police. Critics say this form of punishment is unlikely to succeed in changing the behavior of repeat offenders because those people are used to breaking society's rules anyway.

Asset forfeiture

Asset forfeiture consists of the government's seizing of personal assets obtained from or used in a criminal enterprise. For example, an airplane may be seized if it was used in smuggling drugs into the country. Law enforcement usually keeps the assets.

Both **civil** and **criminal forfeiture** are possible. Civil-forfeiture laws empower the government to take property without charging a person with a crime and without a criminal conviction. Property can be seized if police believe it was bought with profits of illegal activity or used to facilitate a crime. Police need only to show probable cause to seize property under civil law. If the owner wants to reclaim seized property, the owner usually has to file a lawsuit. At the trial in civil court, the burden of proof rests on the owner to prove the property is innocent by a preponderance of evidence — a higher standard than the probable cause standard used to take the property.

The differences between civil and criminal forfeiture are that criminal forfeiture arises *after* the criminal conviction of a defendant and that a defendant in a criminal case is afforded full due process rights. Important parts of the Bill of Rights don't apply to civil forfeiture. For example, the property owner has no Sixth Amendment right to an attorney, no Fifth Amendment right to be protected from self-incrimination, and no Eighth Amendment right to be free from cruel and unusual punishment that is disproportionate to the crime charged against the property. The American Civil Liberties Union believes civil forfeiture violates fundamental constitutional rights, including the right not to be deprived of property without due process of law and the right to be free from punishment that is unreasonably harsh.

Sentencing Statutes and Guidelines

There are three sentencing systems: those featuring determinate-sentencing statutes; those using indeterminate-sentencing statutes; and those applying sentencing guidelines. Some overlap exists among the categories. For example, a mandatory sentence is considered a type of determinate sentence. Mandatory sentencing may be used in jurisdictions that also use indeterminate sentencing as well as in those that use sentencing guidelines.

Drafters of any sentencing law must grapple with the problem of **sentencing disparities,** inconsistencies in sentencing offenders in which those committing the same crime receive different sentences. Sentencing disparities are usually based on race, gender, region, or socioeconomic status. Within academic circles, a debate rages over the effects of race on sentencing. A recent review of 38 studies published since 1975 reports that many of the studies concluded that race had a direct effect on the **in-out decision** (in other words, the decision concerning whether the offender should be punished in a penal institution or out in the community) and that this effect remained even after the inclusion of controls for prior record and crime seriousness.

Other researchers claim that race influences sentence severity indirectly through its effect on factors such as bail status, type of attorney, or type of disposition. Researchers have also found that the racial composition of the offender/victim pair may be a better predictor of sentence severity than the race of the offender. For instance, blacks who murder whites are more likely to be sentenced to death than blacks who murder blacks or than whites who murder blacks or whites. Racial and other kinds of sentencing disparities make a mockery of the principle of "equal justice under the law."

Indeterminate sentences
Indeterminate sentencing is a system of sentencing in which a legislature establishes maximum and minimum terms for each crime and a judge makes a discretionary decision as to what the maximum and minimum sentences should be for each convicted offender. For those whose sentence is prison, a parole board determines the amount of time each inmate serves under correctional supervision.

The theory behind indeterminate-sentencing statutes is rehabilitation—the sentence should meet the needs of the individual offender, and the offender should be locked up until there is evidence that he or she has been "cured." In states with indeterminate sentencing, parole boards can release inmates once they have served the minimum part of their sentences. **Good-time laws** further reduce the amount of time served. Good time reduces a portion of an offender's sentence for good behavior while in prison.

The impact of indeterminate sentencing

Benefits of sentence-reduction programs, such as good-time laws and early parole release, include promotion of discipline within prisons (because inmates are motivated to engage in good behavior in order to earn or avoid losing good time) and the reduction of prison overcrowding. Critics complain that most offenders are released from prison before serving their full sentences and that indeterminate sentences produce gross sentencing disparities because they allow judges too much discretion.

Determinate sentences

Disillusionment with rehabilitation in the 1970s led to the adoption of determinate-sentencing laws. **Determinate sentences** require a fixed period of confinement, with possible reduction for parole. A legislature fixes the terms for particular crimes, thus taking away the sentencing discretion of judges. Under determinate sentencing, the judge still makes the decision of whether or not the offender goes to prison, but the decision as to the length of sentence is taken away from the judge. In some instances, inmates sentenced under determinate sentences are still eligible for parole after serving a portion of their terms.

The impact of determinate sentencing

Determinate sentences move power in the sentencing process from judges to prosecutors, increase the likelihood that offenders will be sent to prison, lengthen sentences, increase the proportion of sentences served in prison before release, and contribute to prison overcrowding. Determinate-sentencing laws restrict the early release of prisoners and require offenders to serve a substantial portion of their sentences (usually 85 percent) before they can be released. The **Violent Crime Control and Law Enforcement Act** (1994) requires states that want to qualify for federal financial aid to change their laws so offenders serve at least 85 percent of their sentences.

Mandatory sentences

All 50 states have mandatory-sentencing laws for crimes such as drunk driving, committing a crime with a dangerous weapon, and selling drugs. Such laws deny judges their traditional powers of discretion. Judges can't reduce the term for offenses that carry prescribed mandatory-minimum sentences, and they are restricted from imposing alternative sentences in the community. Mandatory-sentencing laws enhance the power of prosecutors, who decide what charges to file against defendants, and they are popular with politicians because they make politicians appear tough to the public.

Three-strikes-and-you're-out laws

To get repeat offenders off the streets, over 25 states and the federal government have passed **three-strikes laws.** These mandatory-sentencing laws require long sentences of up to life in prison without parole following conviction for a third felony. Major drawbacks of three-strikes laws include the incarceration of many nonviolent offenders who might be better dealt with through less costly community sanctions and the exacerbation of prison overcrowding. In addition, three-strikes laws result in decreases in plea bargains and increases in trials, since defendants feel they have nothing to lose by going to trial. Other consequences include increasing jail overcrowding as three-strike defendants awaiting trial occupy scarce jail space. Finally, the third, and final, strike can be a nonviolent offense (such as marijuana possession), producing a situation in which the maximum sentence of life imprisonment can be disproportionate to the offender's criminal history.

The impact of mandatory sentencing

Because prosecutors and judges often get around them, mandatory minimums lack predictability and certainty. The U.S. Sentencing Commission reported in 1991 that 40 percent of the federal offenders whose crimes should have triggered mandatory-minimum sentences were able to avoid these sentences. Prosecutors can avoid mandatory minimums by entering into certain kinds of plea bargains. Federal law, for example, allows prosecutors to ask for sentences below the mandatory minimum for defendants who cooperate by providing evidence against other criminals. The enactment of mandatory-sentencing laws also has resulted in the government's having to spend millions of additional dollars to keep more offenders locked up longer.

Sentencing guidelines

By 1998, 17 states and the federal government had adopted sentencing guidelines. These guidelines shift sentencing power from state judges to legislators. To determine the proper sentence, judges follow a grid, which identifies what the proper sentence is for a person who has committed a specific crime and who has a certain criminal history score (based on the number and severity of prior criminal convictions). Congress passed the **Federal Sentencing Guidelines Act** in 1984, which eliminated parole for federal prisoners, limited early release from prison for good behavior, and curtailed the discretion of federal district court judges. Neither federal nor state judges can deviate from sentencing guidelines except when there are aggravating or mitigating circumstances that are not adequately covered in the guidelines. After making such departures from the guidelines, judges must justify them in writing.

The impact of sentencing guidelines

Advantages of guidelines include an opportunity to reduce sentencing disparities, the potential for ensuring rationality in sentencing (for example, making sure that violent crimes are punished with the most severe penalties), and a chance to alleviate prison overcrowding by calibrating the guidelines in a way that reserves prison space for offenders who have committed serious crimes or who have a long history of criminal involvement.

But sentencing guidelines vary, and not all guidelines yield the same benefits. The federal sentencing guidelines, for example, have been subjected to sharp criticism. Lynn Branham, a research scientist at the University of Illinois, claims the federal guidelines are based on the assumption that incarceration is the only fitting punishment tough enough for offenders. Consequently, federal prisons are filled with nonviolent offenders, many of whom could be punished more cheaply and more effectively in community sanctions. Branham also points out that the federal guidelines were drafted without an appreciation that prison space is an expensive, limited resource. As a result, the federal prison population has exploded and taxpayers have been forced to carry the economic burden of building and maintaining the new prisons needed to accommodate the influx of prisoners.

Great Debates in Criminal Justice: Should the Death Penalty Be Abolished?

Few areas of criminal justice have sparked as much debate as the death penalty. The public strongly supports the death penalty even though there are strong arguments suggesting that it should be abolished.

Capital punishment should be abolished

Critics of capital punishment put forward several arguments.

1. The application of the death penalty is so arbitrary that it violates the Eighth Amendment's prohibition against cruel and unusual punishment. Justice Harry Blackmun claims there is an irreconcilable conflict between two requirements in capital sentencing. On the one hand, the Eighth Amendment demands that sentencing discretion in capital cases be structured according to fixed, objective standards to eliminate arbitrariness and discrimination. On the other hand, there is a humanitarian requirement that sentencing discretion be flexible enough to permit sentencers to individualize justice by taking mitigating circumstances into account that might justify a sentence less than death.

2. The death penalty discriminates against racial minorities and the poor. Statistics show that the death penalty is administered in a selective and racially discriminatory manner.

3. The death penalty doesn't deter crime.

4. The death penalty costs taxpayers more than life imprisonment.

5. The inevitability of factual, legal, and moral errors results in a system that must wrongly kill some innocent defendants.

6. Public support for the death penalty diminishes substantially when the public is fully informed about the penalty, the alternative of life imprisonment without parole, and the consequences of the death penalty.

Capital punishment should not be abolished

Proponents of the death penalty make arguments centering around the justifications of fairness, retribution, deterrence, economy, and popularity.

1. The death penalty isn't arbitrary. In ***Gregg v. Georgia*** (1976), the Supreme Court ruled that the death penalty isn't cruel and unusual punishment and that a two-part proceeding — one for determining innocence or guilt and one for determining the sentence — is constitutional. Any conflicts between eliminating arbitrariness and allowing sentencers to individualize justice can be resolved, according to Justice Scalia, by dispensing with the requirement that sentencers consider an array of mitigating circumstances.

2. The death penalty isn't discriminatory. In ***McCleskey v. Kemp*** (1987), the Court held that statistical evidence of racial discrimination in death sentencing can't establish a violation of the Eighth or Fourteenth Amendments. To win an appeal under the equal protection clause of the Fourteenth Amendment, the Court requires an appellant to prove the decision makers in his or her case acted with intent to discriminate.

3. Executions deter would-be criminals from committing crimes.

4. It is cheaper for the government to kill murderers than to keep them in prison for the duration of their lives.

5. The few mistakes that are made in carrying out the death penalty are offset by its crime prevention and economic benefits.

6. Polls show the vast majority of Americans favor the death penalty for murderers.

7. Society has a moral right to punish the most violent criminals by taking their lives. Some violent criminals are vile, wicked persons who deserve to die.

Evaluating the debate over capital punishment

A substantial body of empirical studies shows that the administration of capital punishment is arbitrary, that the costs of trials and multiple appeals make the death penalty more expensive than housing an offender in prison for life, that the death penalty does not deter violent crime, and that during the twentieth century more than 400 people were erroneously convicted in capital cases.

Although the Supreme Court denied the racial discrimination argument in *McCleskey v. Kemp,* statistical evidence supports the claim that the burden of capital punishment falls upon the poor and the underprivileged. Studies show that a disproportionate number of individuals sentenced to death are members of minority groups and that nearly all individuals on death row are indigents.

The argument that the death penalty should be retained because the majority of the people in the United States want it, equates the numbers in support of a position with the correctness of it. The rightness or wrongness of the death penalty logically is neither helped nor hindered by the numbers in support. Opinions don't logically equate to factual knowledge.

Deciding whether or not society has a moral right to take the lives of murderers and other violent criminals requires a value judgment. In support of their position, proponents of the death penalty cite the Judeo-Christian tradition of "eye for eye, tooth for tooth." Opponents counter by emphasizing New Testament admonitions to "turn the other cheek" and "to love thy neighbor."

The Quakers built America's first prison at the end of the eighteenth century. Their motives were altruistic—they sought a humane alternative to corporal punishment and capital punishment. The Quakers' original intent was to rehabilitate inmates through hard work, Bible study, and penitence. Today, more than 200 years later, the Quakers' goal of rehabilitation has been overshadowed by what some policymakers call more realistic goals—deterrence, retribution, and incapacitation.

Prisons

With almost two million inmates populating jails and prisons in the U.S. and billions of taxpayers' dollars being spent on prisons each year, corrections has become a growth industry. Government leaders, eager to respond to public fears of crime, have charted a course that experts project will result in the imprisonment of more than three million people by 2010. Strict sentencing laws and large appropriations for prison construction have forced states and localities to make trade-offs between prisons and education or other services. Proponents of imprisonment hold the view that incarceration is responsible for declining crime rates.

Types of prisons
In the United States, prisons have traditionally been distinguished by custody level.

- **Super-maximum-security prisons** confine the most serious escape and assault risks.

- **Maximum-security prisons** are walled fortresses that hold the most dangerous prisoners.

- **Medium-security prisons** are facilities secured by a series of fences and enclosures that hold inmates considered less dangerous and escape prone than those in maximum-security prisons.

- **Minimum-security prisons** are institutions without walls, without armed guards, and often without perimeter fences and that hold inmates considered to be low security risks.

- **Women's prisons** are separate maximum-, medium-, and minimum-security prisons that hold only female inmates. During the 1990s, the proportion of women in state and federal prisons increased from 3 percent to more than 6 percent. This increase is a reflection of mandatory-sentencing policies and tougher drug laws. A study of female inmates in 1994 found that a majority of them were serving time for drug and drug-related charges. Men's and women's prisons differ. Men's prisons are bigger and more security-conscious; women's prisons tend to have more fluidity in their prison population, since women tend to serve shorter sentences.

- **Coeducational prisons** operate in a number of states. In these institutions, both male and female inmates eat, work, and study together. The rationale behind these prisons is to provide a more normal social environment that will facilitate the eventual reintegration of both men and women into society.

Growth in the prison population has led to the emergence of **private prisons.** Private corporations claim they can own and operate prisons more efficiently than public agencies can. The Corrections Corporation of America is the nation's biggest commercial operator of jails and prisons. In 1998, it owned and operated 34 prisons and jails and operated 43 other facilities that it didn't own. About 5 percent of the people incarcerated in the United States in 1998 were in commercially operated jails and prisons. Corrections Corporation has benefited from close ties to elected officials, especially those who have championed the idea of contracting out government services to corporations to save money.

A 1996 report to Congress by the General Accounting Office found little evidence of savings, however, saying that one Tennessee prison run by Corrections Corporation saved only about 1 percent as compared with state-run prisons.

Inmates

A common myth is that only dangerous people are sentenced to prison. The truth is that in 1992 violent offenders composed 27.1 percent of all state prison admissions. Property offenders, such as burglars, car thieves, and arsonists, made up 34.1 percent of those sentenced to state prisons, and drug-abuse violators made up another 30 percent. The typical prison inmate is a 30-year-old, uneducated male who was earning less than $10,000 a year prior to his arrest and who has a criminal history that includes previous incarceration or probation. The number of women in state and federal prisons in 1998 rose 5 percent over that in 1997. Women still account for only 6 percent of prisoners nationwide.

Exponential growth in the prison population

The number of prisoners has been growing at an extraordinary pace, up 70 percent between 1990 and 1999. The federal and state prison population stood at 129,453 in 1930. It took almost five decades to double, reaching 329,821 in 1980. Then, it took only a little over one decade to triple, nearing 900,000 in 1992. By June 1998, 1.2 million people were held in state and federal prisons. During the past 20 years, the number of persons in prison has quadrupled, and forecasters predict it will continue to grow.

The level of incarceration

The United States trails only Russia in the percentage of its citizens behind bars. The total U.S. incarceration of 668 people per 100,000 in 1998 was six times to ten times higher than that in most industrial nations. In Russia, 685 people out of every 100,000 are behind bars.

A planned amnesty of 100,000 prisoners in Russia and the expectation of continued increases in the U.S. prison population means the United States will probably become the world's leader in imprisonment by early in the twenty-first century.

Racial disparities

The incarceration rate for black men in 1996 was eight times the rate for white men. These figures unquestionably illustrate racial disparity in the nation's prisons. During the late 1990s, disparities were particularly striking for young men. About 8.3 percent of black men ages 25 to 29 were in prison, compared with 2.6 percent of Hispanic men and 0.8 percent of white men of those ages. African-American men go to prison at a higher rate than any other racial group in the United States and are six times more likely than whites to be incarcerated. In 1998, while African-Americans made up 12 percent of the U.S. population, they constituted over 40 percent of sentenced inmates in state and federal correctional institutions. Whites, who made up about 75 percent of the general population, accounted for just over 30 percent of the state and federal inmates.

Regional disparities

There are also sharp regional disparities in incarceration rates, with southern states having the highest rates and states in northern New England and the northern Midwest having the lowest.

The driving force in the growth of the prison population

In a 1999 study of the factors causing the prison population to expand, Alfred Blumstein, a criminologist at Carnegie-Mellon University, and Allen Beck, a prison specialist at the Bureau of Justice Statistics, estimate that 40 percent of the growth is due to **increases in prison admissions** and 60 percent is attributable to **longer prison sentences** served by inmates. The researchers claim the increase in commitments to prison is because of tougher attitudes toward criminals by both prosecutors and judges. The longer time served, they say, is caused by tougher sentencing laws, longer sentences, and more reluctance by parole boards to grant early release.

An additional factor driving both increases in prison admissions and increases in the lengths of sentences is **the drug war.** Drug offenses are accounting for the greatest share of the increase—30 percent of the new commitments to state prisons. Then, too, drug offenders serve long terms because many of them are sentenced under get-tough antidrug laws. Legislation requiring extremely long sentences for drug crimes is a political phenomenon of the last quarter of the twentieth century. Few politicians have been willing to challenge the "get tough on drug crime" attitudes or to look at the economic and human consequences of long sentences.

Prison overcrowding

A major consequence of the tremendous explosion in the prison population is prison overcrowding. Overcrowding became the norm in America's prisons in the 1990s. At the start of 1995, 39 states were under court orders to correct overcrowding and/or unconstitutional conditions. The federal prison system was 26 percent over its rated capacity in 1995. In many prisons, inmates are double-bunked in small cells designed for one person. Others sleep in dormitories, tents, or trailers. Overcrowding contributes to many problems, including the spread of diseases (such as tuberculosis), prison violence, prisoner lawsuits, and the shortage of resources inside prisons.

The federal and state governments have responded to this problem by building more prisons, stretching the capacity of existing facilities, releasing some inmates early, holding some inmates in local jails, expanding probation and parole caseloads, and broadening the range of criminal sanctions beyond the traditional sentences of prison or probation.

CRIMINAL JUSTICE

Prison programs

Institutional programs include medical services, religious programs, education programs, recreation, prison labor and industry, work release (which involves releasing inmates to work in the community during the day and returning them to prison at night), and rehabilitation (for example, group therapy that is used to address problems of specific types of offenders, such as sex offenders and drug abusers).

In evaluating prison programs, the **principle of less eligibility** comes into play. The public believes inmates should never enjoy a higher standard of living behind bars than free citizens experience outside prison. Based on this principle, many citizens think inmates should be denied access to certain forms of recreation, such as weights, television, and movies. Correctional officers and prison administrators counter by arguing that such activities keep prisoners busy and out of trouble. Rehabilitation programs have aroused even more criticism than recreation programs. Results of evaluations of rehabilitation programs are mixed: some programs work for individual offenders, but, in general, there is no clear-cut evidence that rehabilitation reduces recidivism.

Parole

Supervised release from prison before an inmate serves a full sentence is called **parole.** Parole officers working for parole agencies provide supervision and counseling to parolees. Another agency, a parole board, determines whether inmates should be granted parole and establishes conditions that each parolee must abide by. If a parolee violates any of these conditions or commits a new crime, the parole board can revoke parole and reincarcerate the offender.

The abolishment of parole

By 1999, 15 states and the federal government had taken the politically popular step of abolishing parole boards, a vestige of what some consider as a failed system of rehabilitation. The parole system, an

invention of the nineteenth century, consists of two parts: parole
boards that decide when to release prisoners and parole officers who
supervise convicts after they serve time in prison. Politicians advocating the elimination of parole have witnessed disappointing results.
Three states have had to reinstate parole boards after eliminating
them because rising prison populations forced them to jeopardize
public safety by releasing many offenders early. Court orders requiring states to alleviate prison crowding are one way prisoners are
released early. Another way inmates gain early release is by accumu-
lating extensive good-time credits. The argument against eliminating
parole boards is that, without parole, an inmate's release becomes
automatic once the offender serves a portion of a sentence minus
good time. Under such circumstances it is more difficult for correctional authorities to keep dangerous offenders behind bars.

Prisoners' Rights

The **hands-off doctrine** dominated thinking about correctional law
in America during the nineteenth century. American courts regarded
inmates as "slaves of the state." Judges believed prisoners had no
rights because they had forfeited them as a result of their crimes, and
judges didn't interfere with the administration of correctional institutions because they didn't want to violate the principle of separation
of power (in other words, the courts didn't want to interfere with the
authority of the executive branch to administer prisons).

During the 1960s and 1970s, the courts moved away from the hands-
off doctrine and acknowledged that courts have a duty to resolve constitutional claims of prisoners. The assertiveness of Black Muslim
prisoners in making claims upon the courts and the activist Warren
Court's commitment to protecting the rights of minorities, including
persons accused of crimes and persons convicted of crimes, caused
this shift. In addition, several legal developments also led to the temporary demise of the hands-off doctrine.

In *Monroe v. Pape* (1961), the U.S. Supreme Court ruled that citizens could bring **Section 1983 suits** against state officials in federal courts without first exhausting all state judicial remedies. Section 1983 of the **Civil Rights Act of 1871,** which imposes civil liability on any person who deprives another of constitutional rights, became a vehicle inmates could use to challenge the constitutionality of the conditions of prison life. In another significant case, *Robinson v. California* (1962), the Court extended the Eighth Amendment's prohibition against cruel and unusual punishment to the states.

Today, the Court recognizes that prisoners do have certain rights. At the same time, however, the Court holds that prisoners do have fewer rights than free citizens because taking away rights is a legitimate punishment and because the restriction of rights is necessary to maintain security in prisons. The current trend is back to the hands-off doctrine, with the Rehnquist Court granting correctional officials considerable discretion to decide what restrictions should be placed on inmates.

The right to free speech

The First Amendment provides in part that "Congress shall make no law . . .abridging the freedom of speech." Since 1970, the federal and state courts have extended the right of freedom of speech and expression to inmates, requiring correctional administrators to justify restrictions on these rights. In *Procunier v. Martinez* (1974), prisoners challenged the constitutionality of state regulations covering censorship of prisoner mail on the grounds that they violated the prisoners' free-speech rights. One rule banned letters containing inmates' criticisms of prison conditions. Striking down the state regulations as unconstitutional, the Supreme Court set forth two requirements for future efforts to regulate communications of prisoners. First, restrictions on speech must be justified as being necessary for maintaining security or some other substantial governmental interest. Second, the rules can't stop inmate communications any more than is necessary to protect important governmental interests.

The right to freedom of association

Another right protected by the First Amendment is freedom of association. In *Jones v. North Carolina Prisoners' Labor Union* (1977), the Supreme Court upheld the constitutionality of restrictions on the activities of a prisoner labor union.

The right to freedom of religion

Another First Amendment right upon which much prisoners' litigation has concentrated is freedom of religion. The Supreme Court has declared that inmates do have the right to freedom of religion and that prison authorities must provide inmates opportunities to practice their religious faith.

The right of access to the courts

The right of access to the courts is the most important of all prisoners' rights. **Civil rights suits** filed under Section 1983 of the Civil Rights Act of 1871 have served as the main way for inmates to enforce their constitutional rights. Victories in such lawsuits have produced the right to receive assistance from a jailhouse lawyer (an inmate who provides legal advice to other inmates) and the right to be afforded access to adequate law libraries.

Rights during prison disciplinary proceedings

The Fifth and Fourteenth Amendments guarantee due process to all citizens. How much process are inmates due in disciplinary proceedings? In *Wolff v. McDonnell* (1974), the Supreme Court held that when inmates may lose good time, due process demands that certain procedures be in place so inmates are not arbitrarily deprived of their freedom. Inmates have

- The right to be notified of charges against them before their disciplinary hearings.

- The right to call witnesses to testify at their hearings.

- The right to assistance in presenting a defense (which doesn't, however, include the right to an attorney).

- The right to a written statement explaining the evidence used in reaching a disposition.

- The right to an impartial decision maker.

The right to equal protection under the law

The Fourteenth Amendment guarantees all citizens "equal protection of the laws." The most common equal-protection lawsuit by inmates claims **racial discrimination.** Claims alleging **gender-based discrimination** tend to center on fewer educational and work opportunities afforded to female as compared to male inmates. Courts have ruled that facilities, programs, and privileges provided to female inmates must be substantially equivalent to those provided for male inmates.

The right to privacy

Prisoners have no Fourth Amendment right to freedom from unreasonable search and seizure. Prison officials can monitor prisoners' movements throughout prisons, watch prisoners in their cells, and conduct warrantless searches inside prisons. In *Hudson v. Palmer* (1984), the Supreme Court ruled that prisoners have no reasonable expectation of privacy in their prison cells entitling them to Fourth Amendment protection. The Court has denied prisoners any rights to privacy because of the need for prison authorities to have access to cells and prisoners' personal belongings for security reasons.

Rights in conflict

Some litigation in the right-to-privacy area relates to questions about correctional officers of a gender different from an inmate's searching or observing that inmate in the nude. This type of lawsuit is difficult because it involves conflicting rights and interests—inmates are concerned about their privacy; correctional officers, both male and female, have a right to equal employment opportunities; and prison officials have an interest in making prisons safe and secure. The courts have decided that prisoners' right to privacy is *not* violated by inadvertent or infrequent observation of a nude inmate by correctional officers of the opposite sex but that strip searches can't generally be performed by such a correctional officer.

The courts have wavered in their support of equal employment opportunities. In ***Dothard v. Rawlinson*** (1977), for example, the Supreme Court upheld a regulation prohibiting women from working in maximum-security prisons for men in Alabama. The Court found that this ban on employment of women was permissible because of the risk that male prisoners would sexually assault female correctional officers. In his dissent, Justice Marshall criticized the Court's paternalistic attitude toward women and commented that "once again, the pedestal upon which women have been placed has, upon closer inspection, been revealed as a cage." In Marshall's view, women should be allowed to decide for themselves where they want to work and if they are willing to accept working in jobs with higher risks.

The right to be free from cruel and unusual punishment
The Eighth Amendment prohibits cruel and unusual punishment. Eighth Amendment lawsuits claim problems in medical care, the use of force by correctional officers, the failure of prison officials to protect inmates from attacks by other inmates, and improper conditions of confinement. The Supreme Court has recognized in ***Estelle v. Gamble*** (1976) that the "deliberate indifference" of a governmental official to an inmate's medical needs constitutes cruel and unusual punishment.

A common complaint relates to prison crowding. The Court has declared that the double-celling of prisoners is *not* per se unconstitutional. In ***Bell v. Wolfish*** (1979), the Court declared there is no right of "one man, one cell." Sometimes an inmate sues correctional officials, alleging they have used excessive force. In these cases, the courts consider factors such as the need to use force, the seriousness of the injuries caused by the use of force, and whether or not inmates and staff were in danger.

Rights of probationers and parolees

In *Morrissey v. Brewer* (1972), the Supreme Court identified the rights of parolees facing parole revocation. Among the procedural rights of parolees in such a situation are the following:

- The right to attend a preliminary hearing to decide if there is probable cause that the inmate violated conditions of parole.

- The right to advance notice of the preliminary hearing.

- The right to cross-examine adverse witnesses.

- The right to a neutral decision maker.

- The right to receive a written statement describing the evidence relied on and the reasons for revoking parole.

In *Gagnon v. Scarpelli* (1973), the Court granted probationers the same protections, before their probation is revoked, as are outlined in *Morrissey*.

Rights upon release

When inmates are released from prisons, legal obstacles block their successful reentry into society. Ex-felons are often, for example, prohibited from voting, working in certain jobs, and serving on juries. A punishment known as "civil death" involves the termination of all civil rights of convicted felons. No state uses civil death today.

Voter disenfranchisement is the greatest civil penalty imposed on ex-felons. According to a study completed in 1998, 14 percent, or one in seven, of the 10.4 million black males of voting age in the United States are either currently or permanently barred from voting due to a felony conviction. This disenfranchisement is a direct effect of racial disparity in incarceration. Currently, all but four states prohibit inmates from voting while they are in prison. In 13 states, most, although *not* all, felony convictions result in the loss of voting privileges for life.

The tradition of voter disenfranchisement dates back to just after the Civil War when Southern conservatives gathered at state constitutional conventions. Representatives adopted an array of voting barriers, including literacy and property tests and poll taxes. The purpose of voting restrictions was to disenfranchise as many blacks as possible without violating the Fifteenth Amendment. While a century has passed since these conventions, criminal disenfranchisement remains as the only substantial voting restriction of the era still in effect. The cumulative effect of such large numbers of persons being locked out of the electoral process is to dilute the political power of the African-American community.

Megan's law

Many states place extra restrictions on sex offenders. For example, New Jersey passed a special law following the rape and murder of a 7-year-old girl named Megan in 1994. This law requires convicted sex offenders to register with police departments upon release from prison. It also requires police to notify certain people living in the offender's neighborhood, school officials, and the general public of a sex offender's presence in a community. By 1998, more than 40 states had statutes requiring public notification when a sex offender is released into a community. Such laws provide information such as names, pictures, and addresses of sex offenders so parents and teachers can keep guard against reoffending by the sex criminal. The problem is that releasing this kind of information also makes it possible for vigilantes to track down offenders who are living in the community.

Pardons and restoration of rights

How can the negative legal consequences of a criminal conviction be minimized? A **pardon** by a governor or the President removes most or all of the civil disabilities connected to a criminal conviction. A person pardoned for a crime, for example, can vote or sit on a jury. Another way of limiting legal obstacles to reintegration is through the **restoration of rights.** Some states automatically restore rights at the end of incarceration, while other states restore rights only upon application by the offender. Yet another means of limiting the adverse consequences of a conviction is to expunge or seal criminal records. **Expunging** records destroys them, whereas **sealing** limits access to them.

The impact of prisoners' rights lawsuits

Even though prisoners almost never win their lawsuits, these lawsuits have an important impact on prisons. Court decisions in prisoners' rights cases are responsible for better prison living conditions, fairer administrative practices, more access to the courts, more open communication with the outside world, and more opportunities for inmates to practice a variety of religious faiths. Courts have also improved some of the worst conditions in prisons. The downside of prisoners' rights is that the large volume of inmate lawsuits places a burden on the courts.

Great Debates in Criminal Justice: Is Imprisoning More Criminals a Good Way to Prevent Crime?

Policy analysts disagree about whether incarceration is an effective way to reduce crime rates.

Imprisoning more criminals is a good way to prevent crime
Supporters of incarceration make these arguments:

1. Increasing incarceration rates since 1980 correlate with decreasing crime rates and have caused crime rates to decline.

2. The costs of crimes that are prevented through incarceration exceed the costs of building and operating prisons.

3. Prisons reduce crime through incapacitation and deterrence.

4. The public favors get-tough solutions to the crime problem.

Imprisoning more criminals is not a good way to prevent crime.
Critics counter with these arguments.

1. The drop in the crime rate is more a function of small numbers of young males in the 15- to 24-year-old age group than a function of the large number of criminals in jails and prisons.

2. More imprisonment imposes **opportunity costs** (in other words, a tax dollar spent on imprisonment is a tax dollar not spent on education, parks, libraries, recreation centers, highways, universities, and policing) that exceed the costs of crimes prevented by imprisonment.

3. It is appropriate to remove violent offenders from society, but the injudicious use of prison to lock up so many nonviolent offenders (including those convicted of drug possession) undermines family structure by removing a large portion of the males from racial minority communities.

4. The argument that America will be safer if we lock up more criminals ignores research showing that incarceration isn't the most effective way to lower recidivism rates for all offenders. A 1994 Rand study found that community-based drug treatment of cocaine dealers is 15 times more effective than prison in reducing crime by this type of criminal.

---

5. The deterrent effect of imprisonment is overrated. Incarceration fails to deter violent crime because most violent crime is committed impulsively, in the heat of passion or under the influence of drugs. Then, too, the overuse of prison for many small-time drug offenders strips imprisonment of its capacity to scare people into good behavior.

6. Studies indicate the public supports alternatives to incarceration for nonviolent, low-risk offenders. Moreover, a 1995 survey reports that a majority of Americans think drug use can be better handled through prevention and treatment than incarceration.

Evaluating the case for imprisonment of more criminals
It is undeniable that, over recent years, the incarceration rate increased at the same time that crime rate decreased. It is illogical to assume, however, that more incarceration has *resulted* in less crime. It is logical to assume only that the higher incarceration rate and the lower crime rate are concomitant until statistical evidence either proves or disproves the causal effect. Statistically, it is clear that demography (personal circumstances) is more strongly related (although also not necessarily causally) to crime rates than is imprisonment.

Because incarceration is such an expensive solution to the crime problem, the big question remains "Is incarceration cost-effective?" While some studies seem to indicate it is, the lost opportunity costs are staggering. Five states now have a corrections budget of more than a billion dollars per year. Nationwide, spending on corrections at the state level has increased faster than on any other spending category. Corrections expenditures at a national level have risen three times as fast as military expenditures over the last 20 years.

CHAPTER 15
THE JUVENILE JUSTICE SYSTEM

Prior to the 1900s, juvenile lawbreakers were treated like adult offenders. Beginning with the Illinois Juvenile Court Act in 1899, children were treated differently. This Illinois law authorized a separate children's court to hear cases of delinquent, dependent, and neglected children. The invention of the juvenile court was based on the doctrine of ***parens patriae,*** meaning "the state as parent." Bent on saving children from becoming criminals, reformers advocated transferring the responsibilities for protecting children from families to special children's courts. By bringing wayward children under the control of the juvenile court, the court could manage the affairs of children in the manner of a caring father and mother dealing with their children. Undergirding *parens patriae* was the ethnocentric view that many immigrant parents were unsuitable as parents, and this notion, in turn, justified the expanded legal powers of the court.

Juveniles' Responsibilities and Rights

A central premise of the juvenile court is that juveniles and adults should be treated differently. It is assumed that adolescents have less responsibility for their acts and need protection. Therefore, it follows that juveniles should receive less than the full adult penalties for their misconduct. In addition, **informal procedures** are preferred for handling juvenile cases, and **discretionary processes** are the norm. For example, most states have instituted juvenile codes patterned after the Illinois model.

The architects of these laws based their models on the adult criminal court system, while eliminating most of the procedural safeguards protecting constitutional rights of persons accused of crimes. The court was to be paternalistic instead of adversarial. Following

---

the logic of *parens patriae,* it was assumed that formal procedures that ensure constitutional rights for juveniles are unnecessary because the court is committed to looking out for the best interests of children.

Under the *parens patriae* philosophy, the goal of the juvenile court became **individualized justice.** Judges and other decision makers in the juvenile justice system were encouraged to look beyond a youth's alleged crimes to the best interests of the child. Tailoring decisions to the needs of the individual child led them to base discretionary judgments on social characteristics of offenders such as race, sex, age, family status, and social class. Such reliance on nonlegal factors has resulted in differential processing and more severe sentencing of minority youths, raising issues of fairness and equality.

During the 1960s and 1970s, with the due process revolution expanding the rights of adult defendants, the U.S. Supreme Court introduced constitutional due process into the juvenile justice system. More recently, the threat of juvenile crime has led to less emphasis on juveniles' rights and more stress on punishment. As policymakers became disillusioned with rehabilitation, they embraced retribution and deterrence as the best approaches to stopping juvenile street crime. Reflecting this punitive attitude, politicians and the general public demanded that juveniles be tried as adults.

A Separate System

Based on the assumption that juveniles and adults should be treated differently, a separate justice system for juveniles operates in the United States. In 1994, there were more than 2.7 million arrests of persons under age 18. The vast majority of these arrests were for non-violent crimes. About 5 percent were for **status offenses,** such as truancy, running away, or curfew violations.

Juvenile court jurisdiction

The jurisdiction of the juvenile court includes three categories of youths.

- **Delinquents**—youths who commit acts that would be defined as criminal for an adult, including misdemeanors and felonies.

- **Status offenders**—youths who commit acts that would not be defined as criminal if committed by an adult (for example, truancy, running away from home, and curfew violations).

- **Dependent and neglected children**—youths who are deprived and in need of support and supervision.

Nationally, about 75 percent of the cases referred to juvenile courts are delinquency cases (about 1.5 million each year). About 60 percent of these cases involve property crimes. A significant number of cases heard in juvenile court are status offenses.

Age is the most important obvious criterion separating the juvenile court from the adult criminal court. State laws vary in the minimum and maximum age restrictions. Under common law, the minimum age for holding a person accountable for criminal behavior is 7. Maximum age is the age when a person is defined as an adult and no longer subject to the authority of juvenile court. Most states set the maximum age at 17 years of age or below.

Police discretion

Police exercise enormous discretion in dealing with juvenile offenders. They have the following options:

- Release and warn.

- Release and file a report.

- Take the youth to the police station and make a referral to a community youth-services agency.

- Refer to juvenile court intake, without detention.

- Refer to juvenile court intake, with detention.

Over 70 percent of the juveniles who are arrested by the police are referred to the court. But many contacts between the police and juveniles are never recorded because the police handle things informally. For offenses such as curfew violations, running away, and trespassing, the police may warn the youth and/or inform the parents. Sometimes police refer juveniles to social-service agencies, a practice called **diversion,** which removes the juvenile from the juvenile justice system and avoids any negative consequences that might attach to labeling a youth "delinquent."

The most important factor influencing police decisions regarding juveniles is the **seriousness of the crime.** Studies indicate that nonlegal factors such as the youth's race, class, and sex, and the police officer's perception of the youth's demeanor also affect police decision making.

Criminal procedure

In dealing with juveniles, police issue *Miranda* warnings to youths prior to custodial interrogation. On the issue of unreasonable searches and seizures, the U.S. Supreme Court has ruled that school officials can conduct warrantless searches of students and their lockers if they have reasonable suspicion that the searches will yield evidence of school or criminal law violations.

Detention

A police or school referral to juvenile court can be made with or without detention. **Detention** is the temporary jailing of youths who are awaiting disposition of their cases. Most state laws require a **detention hearing** before a juvenile court judge can hear a case. The purpose is to decide whether to release the child to his or her parents or retain custody. The major purposes for locking up juveniles in detention centers are

- To secure their presence at court proceedings.

- To hold those who can't be sent home because parental supervision is lacking.

- To prevent them from harming themselves and to prevent crimes **(preventive detention).**

- To punish.

Who are the youths in detention? About 500,000 juveniles are now detained each year, and the number of juvenile detainees increased steadily during the 1990s. About two-thirds of the juveniles in detention are awaiting adjudication.

Overcrowding is the norm. Conditions in juvenile detention centers are poor, and abuse is often reported. Overcrowding got so bad in New York City in 1998 that officials began detaining boys as young as 10 on a barge anchored in the East River, a few hundred yards from Rikers Island. Child-welfare advocates criticized using the barge because its layout made it difficult to segregate newly arrested children from convicted youths awaiting transfer to juvenile prisons. Without a doubt, many youthful detainees could be supervised in the community without jeopardizing public safety.

Not all juveniles go to detention centers. Some are housed in **adult jails.** The mixing of juveniles and adults in adult jails is considered unjust and remains a problem. Since the 1970s, the juvenile justice system has sought to place juveniles in separate facilities to shield them from the **criminogenic** influences (those tending to produce crime or criminals) of older, adult offenders. Removing children from jails is an ongoing reform initiative. The **Juvenile Justice and Juvenile Delinquency Prevention Act** (1974) requires the removal of status offenders from the juvenile justice system. It also mandates the detaining and incarcerating of juvenile offenders in separate facilities from adults. (Note that the two major points of the law should be understood independently. Remove juveniles who have committed status offenses from the juvenile justice system, and remove most juvenile offenders from adult jails.)

Unlike adult court, the juvenile justice system doesn't provide bail or release on recognizance. In most states, the child must be released to the guardianship of parents or relatives, who must assume responsibility for the child. Many states deny juveniles the right to bail.

Intake

If the police decide to refer a youth to juvenile court rather than handle the case informally, the case goes to a probation officer working in an intake unit of the juvenile court. The major function of intake is to decide whether a **petition** should be filed against a juvenile. In making the intake decision, a probation officer determines whether there is probable cause to believe the accused youth committed a crime. The intake officer exercises considerable discretion in making this decision. The seriousness of the current offense and prior criminal record weigh heavily in intake.

If the probation officer does *not* recommend a petition, the officer can dismiss the charges, place the child on **informal probation,** or refer the child to a community agency. Under informal probation, either the police or a probation agency supervises the youth for a period of time and monitors the youth to make sure he or she complies with conditions of probation. If the youth violates any of the conditions of probation, an intake officer can file a petition for the original offense and refer the case to juvenile court.

The filing of a petition both signifies that there is enough evidence supporting the charges against a youth to warrant further court processing and authorizes a hearing before a juvenile court judge. Each year, about a half million to a million court referrals result in the filing of a petition.

Certification

In 1994, over 12,000 delinquency cases were moved to adult criminal court by a process called **certification** (waiver of jurisdiction). State and federal statutes specify the age of young offenders (usually 16 or 17) at which criminal courts have jurisdiction and provide for waiver. The decision as to whether to transfer a case is made by a juvenile court judge at a **transfer hearing.**

In some states, waivers can apply to juveniles age 16 and over regardless of offense. In other states waivers can occur only for felonies. The effect of a waiver is to deny a juvenile the protection of the juvenile court and to subject the juvenile to the possibility of receiving harsh punishment. The Supreme Court ruled in **Stanford v. Kentucky** (1989) that the death penalty can be imposed for crimes committed by juveniles as young as 16.

Adjudication in juvenile court

During an **adjudication** (or fact-finding) **hearing,** a juvenile court judge decides whether or not there is proof beyond a reasonable doubt to label a youth "delinquent." Rights afforded to juveniles include

- The right to notice of charges.

- The right to counsel.

- The right to confront witnesses.

- The right to cross-examine witnesses.

- The privilege against self-incrimination.

Juveniles have no right to a jury trial. Whereas in adult criminal courts hearsay is inadmissible, there are no similar restrictions on the introduction of hearsay in juvenile courts. While adult criminal trials are open and formal, juvenile hearings are closed and informal. *Parens patriae* is the basis for denying juveniles full constitutional protections. Although supporters of the juvenile court argue that there is no need for such protections because the juvenile court is set up to protect children, these protections are not built into the juvenile court process.

Disposition

If a judge finds a youth delinquent, a **disposition hearing** (which is similar to a sentencing hearing) is held. The purpose is to determine whether the youth is to be put on probation or placed in an institution. About half of the states grant judges the power to sentence youth to an indefinite period of confinement lasting until the youth reaches majority age. More than 80 percent of the adjudicated delinquents get probation. At any given time, more than 500,000 youths are on probation. Besides probation, judges have a variety of other community-based correctional dispositions (for example, halfway houses and foster homes) to choose from.

Institutionalization

More than 100,000 juveniles were serving time in America's juvenile institutions in 1998. A juvenile court can commit a delinquent to a state training school, a ranch, a private residential treatment facility, or a juvenile prison. **Training schools** exist in every state except Massachusetts, which abolished them in the 1970s. Most hold serious delinquents. Almost all are state operated and controlled. To better handle violent youths, some states have created more secure facilities called **juvenile prisons.**

Some of the worst conditions in juvenile corrections can be found among the growing number of **privately operated prisons,** whether those built specifically for one state or those that take juveniles from across the country. Only 5 percent of the nation's juvenile prisons are operated by private, for-profit companies. As their numbers grow, however, their regulation has become one of the hottest issues in juvenile justice. In April 1998, Colorado officials shut down a juvenile prison operated by the Rebound Corporation after a mentally ill 13-year-old's suicide led to an investigation that uncovered repeated instances of physical and sexual abuse. This private prison housed offenders from six states. In July 1998, the Juvenile Justice Project of Louisiana, an offshoot of the Southern Poverty Law Center, filed a federal lawsuit against a private prison for juveniles in Tallulah, Louisiana, to stop brutality and neglect.

Recognizing the problem of cruel and inhumane conditions in juvenile prisons, the U.S. Department of Justice began a series of investigations into state juvenile systems. In a recent investigation of Georgia's juvenile correctional institutions, the DOJ threatened to take over the state's juvenile system, charging a "pattern of egregious conditions violating the federal rights of youth," including the use of pepper spray to restrain mentally ill youths, a lack of textbooks, and guards who routinely stripped young inmates and locked them in their cells for days. In November 1998, the DOJ sued the state of Louisiana, believed to have the worst juvenile prisons in the nation, with failing to protect youthful inmates from brutality by guards and providing inadequate education and medical and mental health care.

A series of Supreme Court decisions and state laws have mandated a higher standard for juvenile prisons than for adult prisons. There is supposed to be more schooling, medical care, and security because the young offenders have been adjudicated delinquent rather than convicted of crimes as adults and therefore are held for rehabilitation rather than punishment. Critics contend that some private prisons, to earn a profit, scrimp on money for education and mental health treatment in states that already spend little in those areas. Critics also assert that these prisons keep staff wages and inmate services at a minimum while taking in as many young inmates as possible.

After institutionalization

The postincarceration stage involves **parole.** A parole officer supervises youthful offenders in the community. Young parolees can have their paroles revoked and be returned to institutions. Juvenile parolees

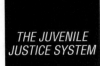

have no due process rights in parole revocation. Parole and other after-care programs are supplemented with electronic monitoring, treatment, education, work training, and intensive parole supervision.

Minorities in Juvenile Justice

There is national concern about the overrepresentation of minority youth confined in correctional facilities in the United States. Research focuses on the extent to which the problem is attributable to

- Minority youths' being more involved in crime.
- A juvenile justice system that treats minority youths and white youths differently.
- A combination of these two factors.

Race effects on juvenile justice in Florida

In a study of the ethnic and racial bias in Florida's justice system covering the period 1985 to 1987, Charles Frazier and Donna Bishop found that nonwhites were more likely than whites to be referred by intake for formal processing, to be held in detention, to be petitioned to court by prosecutors, and to be incarcerated in correctional institutions. After the researchers introduced controls for age, gender, seriousness of the referral offense, and seriousness of their prior records, they still found significant race effects.

Bias against youths of color in Michigan

Madeline Wordes and Tim Bynum collected data from police case files from nine jurisdictions in Michigan in 1990. The data reveal that race/ethnicity played a significant role in police officers' decisions

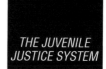

about referral and custody. Controlling for offense seriousness and prior offenses, researchers discovered that black youths were more likely to be referred to court and to be detained.

Racial disparities in Minnesota's juvenile courts

In a study using cases processed through Minnesota's urban juvenile courts in 1986, Barry Feld chastised the juvenile justice system's emphasis on individualized justice for "subjectiveness, arbitrariness, and discrimination." His findings show that urban black youths were at greater risk for pretrial detention, which prejudiced later dispositions, as well as at greater risk for home removal.

Race in juvenile justice in Pennsylvania

Comparing the juvenile justice experiences of white, Latino, and black youths in Pennsylvania in 1989, Kimberly Kempf-Leonard and Henry Sontheimer found that both black and Latino youths were more likely than whites with the same offenses, prior records, and school problems to have their cases processsed through the juvenile court and to be detained.

Overrepresentation of minority youths in the California juvenile justice system

James Austin's 1989 study of the state with the nation's highest rate of youth incarceration documented that, after accounting for factors such as offense and prior record, African-American youths were overrepresented at all decision points in the juvenile justice system from arrest to commitment to the authority of the California Youth Authority.

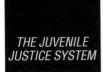

Causes of overrepresentation and solutions to the problem

If the United States is to ensure equality and fairness in the process of both white and minority youths, it must focus on ways to prevent juvenile crime and on approaches to eliminate **system bias** that affects decisions involving juveniles. **Institutional racism** within the juvenile justice system is a primary cause of the overrepresentation of minorities. For example, one instance of system bias is the perception that black families are weaker and less able to provide supervision than white families. Nonwhite youths and their families are less likely to possess the **social and economic resources** (for example, the ability to retain private counsel and get favorable plea bargains) that are available to whites. **Poverty** and **unemployment** are also partly to blame for the differential involvement of minority youth in crime and their high incarceration rates.

Possible solutions include

- Recruiting more racial/ethnic minorities for jobs in law enforcement, probation, and court agencies that operate within the juvenile justice system.

- Instituting cultural sensitivity training for police officers, probation officers, judges, and other key decision makers in juvenile justice.

- Creating employment programs as alternatives to drugs and gangs for minority youths.

- Developing guidelines to aid decision makers in reaching decisions and to ensure equity in processing.

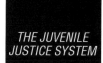
Myths About Juvenile Justice

The belief that youths are becoming more violent and criminally dangerous
Historically, juvenile violent crime arrest rates rose 5.2 percent from 1987 to 1989, 12.1 percent from 1989 to 1990, 7.6 percent from 1990 to 1991, and by at least 4 percent in every year thereafter until 1994. Recently, however, juvenile violence has declined. Arrests for violent crime among juveniles aged 10 to 17 dropped nationally by almost 3 percent from 1994 to 1995. Although juvenile crime now appears to be on the decrease, lawmakers have passed tough laws enabling states to try more juveniles as adults.

New studies call the existence of the new laws into question. One study shows that virtually all the increase in homicides by juveniles in the late 1980s was attributable to crimes committed with **handguns,** not to the emergence of a new breed of superpredator teenagers. While the rate of gun killings by juveniles tripled from 1986 to 1993 and has fallen since, the rate of homicides by juveniles with other weapons has not changed.

New research on juvenile violence also suggests that much of the increase in arrests of juveniles in aggravated assaults in the late 1980s was not because teenagers were more violent, but the result of **increased police activity,** as officers arrested young people in altercations that would have been ignored earlier. Franklin Zimring, director of the Earl Warren Legal Institute at the University of California at Berkeley, claims that reclassification by the police of juvenile fights into aggravated assaults created a completely artificial juvenile crime wave. "Youth in 1998," according to Zimring, "are no more prone to violence than were teens 20 years ago."

But Alfred Blumstein, a criminologist at Carnegie-Mellon University, warns that homicides by juveniles remained higher in 1997 than they were in the early 1980s before the advent of crack cocaine, semiautomatic handguns, and gangs ignited an increase in killings by teens. The rate of homicide by juveniles 14 to 17 years old increased from 8.5 per 100,000 in 1984 to 30.2 in 1993 and then declined to 16.5 in 1997, according to James Alan Fox, dean of the College of Criminal Justice at Northeastern University.

Nevertheless, Zimring argues that most people don't understand that the increase, and more recently, decrease, really involves the role of handguns and not evidence of a violent new breed of teenagers. Since the police in many big cities have begun aggressive programs to take guns away from juveniles, the juvenile homicide rate has dropped.

The belief that locking up more juveniles is cost-effective

Today, conservatives favor a host of reforms that would boost the number of youths incarcerated. These include

- Replacing the juvenile court's rehabilitation philosophy with a get-tough policy that makes the punishment fit the crime.

- Passing mandatory-sentencing laws for juveniles charged with violent crimes and drug crimes.

- Building more juvenile correctional institutions.

Critics of institutionalization think it costs too much and produces more hardened criminals. Reformers favor removing all but the violent juveniles from juvenile facilities and placing them in community programs. **Deinstitutionalization** consists of providing programs in communities instead of institutions. Advocates of deinstitutionalization contend it is more humane, cheaper, and more effective in reducing delinquency than is institutionaliztion.

Studies of the **Massachusetts deinstitutionalization experiment** have identified positive results. In the early and mid-1970s, Jerome Miller, an advocate of reform in juvenile justice, helped several states deinstitutionalize their juvenile justice systems. In Massachusetts, the governor replaced all the reform schools with some 200 different nonprofit programs, including group homes and individual intensive treatment for the worst cases. Researchers found that a decade after Massachusetts closed its reform schools, the recidivism rate was much lower than in states that continued to rely on reform schools and prisons. In Massachusetts, 24 percent of juveniles who had been released for 36 months were reincarcerated or recommitted. In contrast, Texas had a recidivism rate of 43 percent and California a rate of 62 percent. Moreover, when Massachusetts juveniles committed new crimes, the violations were less serious than those by offenders in states with stricter laws. According to Miller, the deinstitutionalization movement was successful—the reforms didn't cost any more than institutionalization, produced lower recidivism rates, and "spoke to civility and decency."

The belief that boot camps "shock" youthful offenders out of their criminal ways

Boot camps are short-term, institutional programs that feature tough physical training to develop discipline and respect for authority. Some programs also provide education, job training, and rehabilitation. Evaluations have revealed that boot camps don't reduce recidivism rates and don't automatically reduce prison overcrowding. Defenders applaud the strict discipline and military-type approach to punishment, but critics point to cases in which workers at boot camps have abused inmates. Five workers at Boys Ranch, an Arizona boot camp for juvenile delinquents, were indicted for murder in a boy's death in 1998. California and Arizona investigators found a pattern of abuse after a 16-year-old youth died after forced exercise.

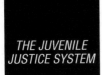

The belief that youths join gangs for protection from neighborhood violence

Youth gangs have become a serious and growing problem in the United States. The need for physical safety and protection is only one reason for joining a gang. Other reasons include a search for a sense of belonging, the need for recognition and power, excitement, and the desire for a sense of self-worth and social status. The problem with youths joining gangs for protection is that it distorts our thinking about gangs. "Kids who join gangs for status or protection usually end up getting in more trouble," says Irving Spergel, a professor at the University of Chicago. "Kids who manage to avoid gangs have found their self-esteem elsewhere." A 1998 Department of Justice study supports Spergel. It found that those who join gangs for protection often suffer serious brutality in the assaults that are part of gang initiation rites. This study also found that gang members were more likely to commit crimes involving drugs, auto theft, and shootings than their nongang peers. Gang members are also more likely to possess weapons. According to Spergel, the best single predictor of kids' avoiding or getting out of gangs is their finding legitimate employment.

The belief that there is an emerging consensus about how to deal with juvenile delinquency

In reality, there are big differences of opinion on how to deal with delinquents. Do we punish them, as most Americans want to do, or do we treat and rehabilitate them? For the past century, since the creation of the first juvenile court in Chicago in 1899, the main goal of the juvenile justice system has been to protect and rehabilitate young offenders. Public policy is now moving away from that ideal, as we seek to put more juveniles in adult court and incarcerate them in adult prisons.

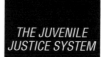

Fox Butterfield, an expert on juvenile justice, claims this emerging policy flies in the face of research showing that while some very young violent children are almost impossible to reform, a large number can be helped. According to Butterfield, the costs of early intervention may be lower than those associated with incarceration. Head Start and infant home visitation programs with trained nurses or social workers, family therapy and parent training, and life skills training (which teaches stress management, problem-solving, and self-control) have potential for reducing delinquency and cost less than simply building more juvenile and adult prisons.

Great Debates in Criminal Justice: Should the Juvenile Courts Be Abolished and Juvenile Offenders Be Tried as Adults?

Since the juvenile court was started more than a hundred years ago, a basic assumption underlying the juvenile court has been that juvenile offenders shouldn't go through the adult criminal courts. The juvenile court was created to handle juvenile offenders on the basis of their youth rather than their crimes. The purpose of juvenile court is treatment and guidance rather than punishment. During the 1980s and 1990s, the public called for getting tough with juveniles and trying them as adults. Many states passed laws making it easier to try certain youthful offenders as adults; some states considered the radical proposal of abolishing juvenile courts.

Juvenile courts should be abolished
Supporters of getting rid of juvenile courts center their arguments on the need to punish juvenile criminals and a concern for juveniles' rights.

1. The juvenile court is founded on false premises because its purpose is to shield youths from the consequences of their own actions.

2. The juvenile court fails to deter juvenile violence.

3. The current juvenile crime problem requires that we punish juvenile offenders in order to deter the next generation of juveniles from becoming predators.

4. Justice demands that juvenile courts be abolished—if juveniles are tried in adult courts, they will be afforded their full array of constitutional rights.

Juvenile courts should not be abolished
Many experts believe abolishing the juvenile court will only make matters worse.

1. The premise of the juvenile court is sound—since children have not fully matured, they shouldn't be held to the same standards of accountability as adults.

2. The purpose of the juvenile court is to treat, not to deter.

3. Changing the social environment in which juveniles live is a more effective way to reduce juvenile violence than punishing juvenile offenders in adult courts.

4. While the denial of full constitutional rights for juveniles is sometimes a problem, the juvenile court's mission is benevolence—to serve the best interests of children.

Evaluating the case for abolishing juvenile courts
It has been suggested that the entire debate over whether or not to abolish the juvenile court diverts attention away from the most important question confronting the juvenile justice system: How can juvenile

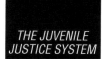
delinquency be reduced when neither the present juvenile courts nor adult criminal courts are designed to attack the various environmental factors that are among the causes of juvenile violence?

The initial causes of much juvenile crime are found in the early learning experiences in the family. They involve weak family bonding and ineffective supervision, child abuse and neglect, and inconsistent and harsh discipline. In addition, there are indications that very poor urban communities put youths at greater risk for involvement in violence. Some neighborhoods also provide special opportunities for learning or participating in violence.

The presence of gangs and illegal drug markets provides exposure to violence, negative role models, and possible rewards for youthful involvement in violent criminal activities. Schools also play a part in generating juvenile violence. An important cause of the onset of serious violent behavior is involvement in a delinquent peer group. Alcohol and guns are also implicated in violent behavior by juveniles. In addition, growing up in poverty and unemployment have major effects on the likelihood that a young person will turn to violence during the transition to adulthood.

From a public policy standpoint, several strategies other than incarceration have been proposed for preventing serious juvenile crime:

1. Make youth access to handguns harder and make guns safer as a way of reducing gun-related crimes by juveniles.

2. Improve schools serving juveniles living in poor urban communities.

3. Provide parents with the skills and resources to show their children unconditional love in safe settings in order to reduce child abuse and neglect.

4. Create meaningful job opportunities and employment training programs to attack poverty.

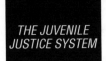

Notes

_____

_____

_____

_____

_____

_____

_____

_____

_____

_____

_____

_____

_____

_____

_____

_____

_____

_____

_____

_____

_____

_____

Notes

Notes

Notes

Notes

_____
_____
_____
_____
_____
_____
_____
_____
_____
_____
_____
_____
_____
_____
_____
_____
_____
_____
_____
_____
_____
_____
_____
_____
_____

Notes